MAMA LOVED
KERRY
DRAKE

PALMETTO
PUBLISHING

Charleston, SC
www.PalmettoPublishing.com

Mama Loved Kerry Drake
Copyright © 2022 by Kerry Lyle

First Edition

Paperback ISBN: 979-8-88590-785-9

Kerry Lyle

MAMA LOVED KERRY DRAKE

KERRY DRAKE

INTRODUCTION

This is a fictional story intended to give us all a break from the personal, state, national and world events in our lives today. Here we have a baby boy who is born into a loving family when our nation is at war against socialist dictators. These are the musings, actions and reactions of that boy who is in, what some of us might think of as, a bygone era. Here is a narrative through the eyes of a boy growing up in a post-war time that was new to us all. Now possibly, because he was the baby of what today would be considered a large family, he was somewhat allowed to roam about and experience things on his own (He couldn't be watched all the time). Of course, he would then suffer, or enjoy, the consequences of these experiences. This story contains some colloquial and archaic words and phrases that may have been used during this time period and, are intended for humor only in order for some of us to relate to the time. My hope is that you may be able to connect with the meanderings of this young boy in his experiences and that you will enjoy them yourself. So, here we go. Hope you enjoy and thank you so much for taking the time.

MAMA LOVED KERRY DRAKE

(As an aside) *Kerry Drake* is the title of a comic strip about a detective created for Publishers Syndicate by Alfred Andriola as artist and Allen Saunders as uncredited writer. It debuted on Monday, October 4, 1943, and was syndicated continuously through June 26, 1983. [1]

Table of Contents

Chapter One

It's All in The Name

(Screaming in pain) EIIIIIIIIIIEEEEIIIEEEIIIEEE!

Melba was nine months pregnant with her eighth child and was having regular, strong labor pains. Sadly, her first two babies had passed away very early in life.

However, at this time, most of her attention was on the Sunday newspaper comic strips and her fanatical attraction to, Kerry Drake.

(Screaming in pain) EIIIIIIIIIIIEEEEIIIEEEIIIEEE!

"Melba!!"

"You better get in here on this table right now or you're going to have that baby right there on that couch," hollered her mama. (All us children were born at home, and most of us on the dining room table." Melba's mama was also the mid-wife.

"I'll be there in a minute," Melba screamed back. "You know I have to see what happened to Kerry. That crook, Bottleneck, has stolen a car, killed the owner and is speeding down the highway with Kerry right behind him."

"Well, your baby is going to go speeding somewhere else if you don't get in here," replied her mama. "Vernon you, and Junior, better get in there and drag her out here. We're already going to have a big enough mess to clean up, as it is."

"Yes'um," replied Vernon, Melba's husband, as he and their eldest, Vernon Jr., traipsed off to the living room to get her.

They grabbed her under each arm and pulled her up, all the while, she's screaming and carrying on about Kerry Drake.

When they finally got her on the dining room table, which had already been covered over with sheets and blankets well, wouldn't you know it, here comes the baby.

Well, it was the best looking, baby boy you had ever seen in all yore born days. (Later on, everybody from miles around would say those very words.)

So, no sooner had that handsome little boy come out than Granny commenced to asking Mama what she was going to name this Adonis.

Now you got to understand, from the time they grabbed her up by the arms and drug her onto that table, while strugglin', and screaming and carrying on like nobody's business, she was still trying to read about what happened to that Kerry Drake.

And, knowing Granny like I do, she wasn't about to let up on wanting to know what Melba was going to name that Atlas look-a-like. So, Mama, frustrated, still in pain, and still thinking about her hero, just screamed out "KERRY."

......and that's how it came about that I got the name of Kerry.

Well, now if you all would just settle down and listen up, I'll go ahead on and tell you about all (or some) of the twists and turns that have come to make up this life's journey.

Chapter Two

When Vernon met Melba

As fate would have it, I was born at a very early age in the small town of Leeds, Alabama, population around 2,500. When I came along, I made number six in the family, so we were more than a little cramped in that two-bedroom house. Daddy was working literally, from daylight to dark, for the city. He did just about everything you

No. 7 West Mann Rd. 5 - 20

could think of, but mainly he was responsible for all the electrical work. He was real smart like that.

Downtown Leeds, AL

Now I'm not one to brag, but my daddy was a very smart man. Times were very hard in those days and when his daddy died, Daddy had to drop out of school after beginning the twelfth grade. He always did well in school and really excelled in math and science. He was always doing everything he could to make extra money and, very often the principal would ask him to tutor different kids in these subjects. Daddy was always glad to do it.

Daddy was a hard worker. From the time he dropped out of school he did pretty much everything you could think of to bring home money for his mama and two younger brothers and two younger sisters. He would cut people's grass with one of those push mowers that was a lot harder to use than the one's today.

He would run errands for people, go buy groceries for people who couldn't get out, or go pay their bills for them. He also worked part-time at the General

Store there close to home. He did just about anything he could think of. Why, one day he rode a bicycle all the way from Lover's Lane, the street they lived on, clear across town to the train station, to take a lady her suitcase. She had forgotten it at the store. But, wouldn't you know it, she also forgot to pay him. Bless her heart!

Then things began to look up. After a year or so, an opening came up at that general store that was a few blocks from Lover's Lane and Daddy was able to get the job. This store carried just about everything anybody would want or use, from tractors and plows, to thimbles and needles and everything in between. Now Daddy was finally able take care of his family from one job. What a blessing!

Not long after going to work there, Daddy met this young girl named Melba, who had just moved there from Arkansas. She was living with her cousin who was working at the store. Melba got to where she would come into the store every so often. Well, Daddy, who was a little shy, started looking out for when she might come in.

Though Unbeknownst to Daddy, this young girl had told her cousin the first time she saw him that, "He is mine if I never do get him."

Well, the more she came in, the more friendly they got. Finally, one day when she had come in a little late in the day, he asked her if he could carrry her packages home for her when he got off. She said, "OK." Well, that really started something right there.

For a few months he would walk over to her house, which was about a mile from home and they would sit on the porch, or walk to town for a soda, or just walk. His feet and legs got real tired during this time so he figured he'd just ask her to marry him and save a lot of money on shoe leather and leniment. (His younger brothers, Theo and A L, had gotten jobs by this time, and with their two incomes, Daddy no longer had to worry about his mama and twin sisters, Mona and Merna.)

All this time, Daddy was getting real anxious and nervous about asking Melba to marry him. So, one afternoon, on the way home, he just came right out and said, "Melba, for some time now I been walking you home from work every day. I been walking you to town for sodas and walking you to church every Sunday. I been sitting on your porch swing and holding your hand. Now, I got to ask you, don't you smell a rat?"

That was when she said, "Vernon, for some time now you been walking me home from work every day. You been walking me to town for sodas and to church every Sunday. You been sitting on my porch swing and holding my hand. Now, I got to ask you, what took you so long? So, they got married the next week. They moved into this little house and right off started having kids and, all told, they was married for over half a century.

Well, as time went on and they started having babies, Daddy was able to get a better paying job, eventhough it was a much harder working job. It was with the City and had potential. He started out working on the 'street paving and repair gang' and eventually moved on up to electrician. Daddy was real smart like that.

However, as life goes on and all us babies came, the war had gotten real big. Daddy had heard that the federal government had built a military ordnance plant in the city of Childersburg, and the word was that they was still hiring.

So, Daddy asked the principal, and the math and science teachers to write him letters of reference. Well, they gladly did it, so he took a day off from work to go check out the jobs at that plant.

Now, seeing as how we lived right in town, we didn't have a real need for a car. Daddy had just been walking to work, or to the store, or anywhere else for that matter.

So, real early the next morning Mama fixed him a sack lunch and Daddy walked down to the train trestle on the other side of town and caught a ride on the train going to Childersburg.

Now, it was still dark as the train slowly pulled into Childersburg and he hopped off just as it came under the overpass of the road going to the plant. He got up, cleaned himself off best he could, then walked the rest of the way to the plant, which was a good five miles.

When he got there the office had still not opened yet, so he waited with all the other men looking for work. When it opened and he got his turn, they asked him what job he was applying for. Although he would have taken anything, he told them he was an electrician. Well, that got their attention real quick. After filling out all the necessary paperwork, and taking all the tests he was told to, he felt pretty good about it all, so he left there with some confidence. Them govment people was a whole lot nicer that he figured they might be.

But you know, things don't always go just as you plan in this life. Daddy didn't know it, but the train didn't go back to Leeds until the next morning. So, after he walked back to the bridge, he had to spend the night under there in order to catch it as it came back by the next morning. Of course, this caused him to miss another day of work so, when he went to work the next morning, they fired him.

But, hallelujah, the Lord was with him, and Alabama Ordnance Works let him know by telegram that evening that he got the job. He was going to be an electrician. On top of that, it came with a two-story house in the Pine Crest area (government staff housing) and also, they would send a truck to move us.

Boy, don't you know that day there was a lot of jumping around and hollering and hugging like you wouldn't believe. Junior, who was the oldest, was so excited he started talking about quitting school and going to work at the plant, too. That is, until Daddy knocked him down a couple of times.

Oh, I almost forgot to mention, Daddy was able to take that telegram and use it as proof of the job to buy an old used Plymouth (on time of course).

Well, it's easy to see how about that time we was in some mighty high cotton. After all the celebrating that day, with my help, we started doing all we needed to do to be ready to throw it all on the truck and move the next day. When the truck got there early the next morning, we was ready to load up and go.

(Uh wait, I guess you was wondering, that since I was only a kid at that time, what did I mean, "..with my help.") Well, evidently you don't know, or maybe don't remember, just how much help a kid can be. With a family this size, I had been carrying my own weight by feeding and dressing myself for at least a year now.

Chapter Three

The Journey

Hey, before I go any further, I guess I need to fill you in on the rest of the family. Well, first there was Vernon Jr., we just called him Junior. Then after him came Bertha Lou. Then after her it was Lora Lee. After Lora Lee came the twins, Rosa Sharon and Timothy Aaron. Timmy, as we called him, always said that Rosa tried to push him back up in there. Rosa, however, still maintains to this day, that that wasn't her that did that. (We've always been just a little bit cautious of trying to figure that one out.) Then Last, but not least, came the aforementioned Adonis, Kerry. (Everybody from miles around said those very words.)

Meanwhile, as I was saying, we piled as many of us in the car as we could. Daddy was all ready to go when Mama asked where Timmy and Kerry were. Daddy started looking around and hollering for us and there we was, standing right there by his leg all the time. (He was always joking around like that.)

Daddy said since me and Timmy was the last ones born, we would get to ride on the back of the truck.

(Boy, were we excited about that.) We climbed up on the back of that truck with our feet dangling out and sat there just as proud as punch. Mama asked Daddy what would we do if it rained and Daddy told her not to be so negative. I didn't know what that meant but Daddy was always being encouraging like that.

Well, after Daddy told the truck driver that he would honk the horn three quick times if we needed to stop, away we went.

Have you ever noticed? I never knew the people on the highways are so nice. Cars would be going by us with folks honking and waving and hollering at us so friendly like, saying stuff about kids and danger and all. Just being real neighborly. Well, since we didn't want to appear uppity, we just waved right back.

1939 P-8 (Plymouth photo)

Now let me tell you Daddy was real proud of that car, being it was the first one he'd ever owned. As we went along, he would turn the radio on and off and we'd all laugh. Then he would turn the windshield wipers on and off, or turn the light on and off up on the ceiling and we'd laugh some more. He would tap on the breaks a bunch of times making everybody jump back and forth. It was a real fun time.

One time he hit the brakes real hard and threw all of them back there into the back of the front seat. Junior hit his face on the back of Bertha Lou's head, cutting her head with his tooth and causing his nose to bleed. Mama said that was enough playing around. (Daddy was always joking around like that.)

I learned a lot about cars that day from just from riding on the back of that truck. One thing I learned was that cars used more water than they did gas. That's right! I didn't know that either. That was a new thing for me, too. I learned this because we stopped four or five times to fill up that radiator and never did have to stop and get gas. But, Daddy explained that to us. He said the big newer cars had to stop even more than that to fill up their radiators. So, we was lucky we didn't have a new car. Daddy was real good about explaining things that way. He even thought to bring a few extra jugs of water with us.

Daddy told Timmy he could be the lucky one to watch and signal him when the smoke started coming out of the front of the car. That way Daddy would know when to blow the horn three times and stop the car for water. One time I distracted Timmy by telling him his adam's apple was about to stick out through the front of his neck. So, while he was grabbing his neck, I got to be the one to signal Daddy to stop. There's just no two ways about it, it was a fun time.

Well, for the most part the rest of our trip to Childersburg went uneventful. That is, if you don't count the fact that highway 25 coming out of Leeds and going over the mountain was at times a bit scary. There was a couple of times the curves were so sharp Daddy almost ran into the side of us.

Why, I could've jumped right out on the hood of the car. Then, other times, it would be so close to the edge of the mountain a gust of wind would have blown us right off the cliff.

It made you think that just staying in Leeds all the time, it was kind of hard to see what the rest of the world might be like. I mean, just being right there in that one place all the time.

As we drove, there was quite a few men walkin' along the road. Some of 'em thumbing, some of 'em just walking with their heads down. You couldn't help but wonder what they might be thinking about what with it being hard times and all. I'm sure some of 'em had families they was thinking about and all. I think some had probably just come back from the war, judging by the parts of army uniforms they had on. We probably would have stopped and picked some of 'em up if we'd had room, but we didn't, (have room that is). I sure hope they was able to find jobs.

After a few hours we finally got to Highway 280 and then went on to Childersburg. Now let me tell you, when we got to that Coosa River we just had to stop. Daddy blew the horn three times then went up and told the driver to go ahead on to the house. He told them they could eat their lunch there and wait for us.

I don't think the driver minded a bit though, especially after all the stops we'd already had to make for water. He was real nice about it too, even thanked Daddy for letting them know.

Let me tell you that river was the biggest bunch of water us kids had ever seen, and we just couldn't help but stop and gawk. Daddy decided that since we'd already stopped, we would just go ahead and pull over right there and have our picnic lunch that Mama had fixed for us.

But you know, it was good we pulled over when we did. For some reason cars was starting to pile up behind us and blowing their horns and everything. I figure they was just enjoying seeing us have such a good time. We just waved right back at 'em. People on the highways are just so friendly like that.

Well, that was the best lunch we could have had. Potted meat and mayonnaise samiches, and warm milk with Vienna sausages for dessert. You just don't get no better than that. Now let me tell you right there on that river bank was, I think, the best time we had ever had in our whole lives.

I think if we'd had the makin's, we might've just built a lean-to and homesteaded us a place right there on the side of that river. But I guess that's enough dreaming for now.

After eating we just played around a little bit beside the river. Daddy took a nap while Mama cleaned up the mess we made. Junior, he sneaked around behind the car and rolled him a cigarette. While he smoked it, Bertha Lou and Lora Lee did what they always do, fussed and fought about dolls, and clothes, and hair. I don't know why they did that. Didn't neither one of 'em look too purty to me.

While all of that was going on, Timmy and Rosa was carrying on something awful. They had been playing in the water when Timmy pushed Rosa down in the mud and she was covered from head to toe. Well, that did it. Her screaming woke up Daddy and He just picked her up and threw her in the river and told her to wash off.

Well, that got me and Timmy so excited, we got down and started rolling in the mud ourselves. We was hoping Daddy would throw us in the river, too. But wouldn't you know it, that made Daddy even madder, so he  just threw us up on the bank and told us to stay there 'til time to leave. We had to go the rest of the way with the mud drying on us like that.

Since the truck had already gone on, Daddy had to figure out a place to put me and Timmy. He decided that we would have to ride in the trunk of the car. We thought it would be fun to ride back there and watch all the cars come up behind us. But then, we had another problem. The trunk lid kept coming down. Since Timmy was the older of us two, I knew he would have the best idea of what to do. He said that I could stand up and hold up the lid.

However, after even standing on my tip toes, we saw that I was too short for the job. So, Timmy, being the oldest and wisest, decided he would stand out on the bumper and hold up the lid. You should have seen him. I was so proud.

Both feet on the bumper and both hands holding up the trunk lid. Just to be on the safe side, I tied some kite string around him and tied the other end to the spare tire wheel. (It didn't have a tire on it.) I was so proud.

Well, just like before, we took notice right off on how friendly people are on the highways. They kept honking and waving and hollering, bragging on us about safety and such, just like they were kin or something. We wanted to be the same way to them, so we just waved right back. People sure are nice.

Before we pulled out, Daddy had to pour more water in the radiator. He looked like he was growling about something. I think I heard him say something about "radiator" but, I don't know. I figured he had probably just gotten a haircut lately and you know how those little hairs start growing down your neck under your shirt and kind of aggravates you.

Then we got back up on the road and went across the great *Coosa River Bridge*.

Man, what a ride! I believe you could see about a hundred miles on both sides.

Childersburg, here we come!

Chapter Four

Welcome to Childersburg

Now rolling into Childersburg was just like going to see Santa Claus at the *Woolworth's* store in Leeds. To us, it was the most exciting thing since mama ran that underwear salesman off our property with a stick.

Now, here we were. Childersburg, Alabama. The big city. Some day to be recognized as the longest continually occupied settlement in the United States of America. And look at us now.

As we crossed over that beautiful bridge into Childersburg we all started to sing and yell and clap. Then, the first thing we saw was that world famous mainstay of great catfish and steak meals, the *River Terrace Restaurant and Motel*. Just think, I didn't know it then, but someday I would be a classmate of the son of the owner of that restaurant.

The next thing on the right was, our very own prison!!!.
WHAT!! YOU'VE GOT TO BE KIDDING ME!!

We was talking about how exciting it would be if there was an escape. Sirens going off. Guards with machine guns blazing. Prisoners on the lam. APB's, 10-4's, over and outs, and everything. Just like *Mr. District Attorney* on the radio. It reminded us of when we played at home, and I would be *Kerry Drake* and Timmy would be *Bottleneck*.

Then we had to get back to the real life. As we drove on, on the left was a row of white houses owned by a lady named Sheffield. Little did we know at the time how these houses would come to mean something in our future.

Almost immediately, we came to a yellow blinking light. We turned left onto what was called *The Plant Road*. We all wanted to go on into the town, but Daddy said we had to get to the house so the workers could finish moving us in. We then drove up the hill and over the bridge that Daddy had spent the night under.

Timmy was starting to get really tired, so we started hollering for Daddy to stop. Daddy thought we was just playing around, so he didn't stop for a while. When Timmy couldn't hold the trunk lid up any longer, he jumped back into the trunk real quick and just let it slam shut. Boy was it dark in there, not to mention how much it stunk from all the exhaust. It didn't take long for us to start getting sleepy. Luckily, Junior had heard the trunk lid slam and hollered for Daddy to stop. It was a good thing when they let us pile in on them in the back seat.

A little while later, Daddy turned onto the Pine Crest Drive and drove all the way to the end. The drive had

houses on each side and ended in a big circle with houses all the way around.

Would you believe our house was at the very end of that circle. I learned sometime later that is called a "bulb cul-de-sac". In Leeds, we just called'em dead ends.

Well, let me tell you, that house was a site to behold. White, two stories with a full basement.

If you can imagine, we started climbing out of that car in slow motion like we was in a movie, all the while staring up at the house. We had never seen anything like this, except maybe in the movies or funny papers. Mama started crying. I didn't get it, but I have since learned that women are funny like that.

The truck had been backed up in the driveway and was already unloaded, except for the stove and icebox. We wondered if maybe they didn't fit or something. We didn't have that much furniture anyway, leastwise not enough for that house.

The bedroom stuff had been taken upstairs. The kitchen stuff to the kitchen. The living room stuff was taken to, well I guess you've got the picture by now. We figured we probably had the poorest looking, most worn out stuff in the neighborhood.

But you know, we found out later that wasn't altogether true for all of 'em. Some of the people got jobs at the powder plant (That was what it came to be know as.) came from backgrounds similar to ours. As we were moving in, some people was standing out in their yards looking at what we had. Mama and Daddy figured it wouldn't be too long before we would have better stuff.

The reason we had gotten this kind of house, or any kind of house for that matter, was because the job position required it. With the recommendations Daddy had, and after taking and passing all the tests required for the position, he was being hired for 'Shift Electrical Supervisor'. It was a position they needed very badly to fill at the time. The government had very strict requirements as well as enticements for Supervisory personnel.

We learned later that the previous supervisor had not been handling the wiring correctly and had been electrocuted. Daddy said he hated it that he got the job because somebody got killed but, at the same time, he needed it to be able to take care of his family. He said things like that makes a feller wonder.

Chapter Five

The Taj Mahal

Now, let me give you the layout of the land here. Upstairs there were three bedrooms each with a closet. (What!) One bedroom for Timmy and me, one for Bertha, Lora and Rosa, and one for Junior. There was one bathroom with tub/shower and linen closet. (First tub I had ever seen with no rust rings in it.)

Downstairs was a marvel. There was the living room, kitchen, dining room, and a bedroom with a big walk-in closet for Mama and Daddy with another bathroom.

The kitchen already had a brand-new electric stove and an icebox provided. We still called'em iceboxes 'cause the one we had in Leeds you really had to have a block of ice in it. Timmy and Rosa sometimes got to walk down to the ice-house with the wagon to bring back a block or two.

It was supposed to be Bertha's and Lora's job but, they would give them each a nickle to do it for them. Sometimes I got to tag along but I had to promise to stay right with them. One time I got kinda sidetracked and put this stick in a mud puddle for a boat. When

I went to pick it up, I fell over in the mud puddle. I told Mama it was their fault for goin' so fast. That didn't work, though, I still got a whuppin'. Anyway, the men just loaded our old ones back on the truck and took them off with 'em.

The basement was, all together, another world entire. To start with, it had a full concrete floor. There was an electric washing machine with a ringer. I didn't even know what a ringer was. But, I learned the first time Mama did the wash. After you washed the clothes, you just stuck them between the rollers and it wrung the water out for you. (To me, that was *Buck Rogers* space age stuff.)

You did have to be real careful with it, though. The first time Mama used it, she got her hand caught in it and started screaming like crazy.

Before Daddy could snatch out the cord, it had pulled her arm in clear up past her elbow. That would be my first time seeing somebody with a blue arm. Mama screamed and hollered for what seemed like forever. People came back out in their front yards again trying to see what happened.

Let me tell you, Mama was not happy about that machine. She gave that thing a wide berth for a while. When she washed closed she made, who ever was close, put the clothes through that ringer for her. Finally, she got to where she would do it herself, very carefully. One time she caught Daddy laughing and slapped him with a wet brassiere. Daddy didn't laugh any more after that (Leastwise not so's anybody would notice.)

Also, over in one corner of that basement, just as purty as you please, sat a toilet, sitting right out there in the open. Just sittin' there. STRANGE!

I asked why it was just sitting there, right out in the open like that and Mama said it was for emergencies. I asked her if she meant like if the washing machine wasn't working and she said, "I guess."

Well, any way, there was a whole lot of vacant space in that basement for whatever you wanted to put in it. Its amazing how quick you can come up with stuff to put in an empty space like that. But, it didn't take us too long to fill it up.

With my limited number of words there's only thing I can say. We was in the highest cotton you ever saw.

Chapter Six

It Was Huey's Fault

As time went on, we got more and more settled into our new surroundings. We met our new neighbors on the left of us, if you were facing the front or our house. Their name was Cox. The daddy worked at the same plant Daddy worked at. They had a little boy named Huey who was about my age.

When we played together, I tended to get in trouble a lot. It was always his fault, of course. Like when I showed him that curious oddity of a toilet sitting there all alone in our basement. He thought it was funny and laughed so hard I had to hit him. He ran home and told his mama and I got a whuppin'.

One day me and Huey was playing in the basement and I wondered where things went when you flushed that toilet. We wanted to find out real bad so, we used the "flinch test" to see who would stand up in it while the other flushed it. We made a pack, then and there, that the one who got flushed would try, somehow or 'nother to contact the other, from the "other side."

Now for you uneducated folks, the "flinch test" is where you would take turns hitting the other in the arm and the first one to "flinch" would have to be the one to get flushed. Well, I lost.

There was nothin' else to be done, but to stand up in that toilet, shoes and all, and let Huey flush it. Well, I weren't that simple. I bet he flushed that toilet a hunderd times and there I was, still standing there. So, we tried it with my shoes off, but outside of getting my socks wet, that didn't work any better. We'd started out all adventuresome, laughing, excited, and everything. But after a while I started getting tired. I was already starting to hold on to the back of that thing.

Now wouldn't you know it? Mama, thinking I was upstairs asleep, kept hearing the water running. Well, after looking all over the house, she came down to the basement to check it out. When she saw what was going on she got real upset. (You might as well know right now, Mama was prone to getting real upset. Daddy called 'em fits, but not in front of Mama.)

She sent Huey home and grabbed me by the neck and took me upstairs and I got a whuppin'. We never did learn where you would go when you got flushed down that toilet. Mama said, "To hell," but, I still wasn't too sure. The only thing I was sure of at that point was, it was Huey's fault and I got a whuppin'.

Another time Mama and Mrs. Cox was out in their front yard gossipin', uh, I mean talkin'. Mama had told her that I was upstairs asleep. All of a sudden, Huey came running out of their house just a waving his arms and pointing up at our house. They looked up and there I was, purty as you please, just enjoying the lovely neighborhood sitting in the window with my feet dangling out.

Mama was about to scream at me, but Mrs. Cox stopped her. She said, "If you scream now, you might scare him and make him fall out." Well, after tossing it around in her mind back and forth a bit longer, Mama marched right into that house and before I knew it, had come up behind me, grabbed me by the neck, and jerked me back into the room. Just like I told you before, as usual it was Huey's fault and I got a whuppin'.

Chapter Seven

Tennis Ain't All it's Cracked Up To Be!

Then, there was the time, when the folks that do this sort of thing, started building a tennis court in the neighborhood.

They had the asphalt all finished and had brought in the poles for the lights. They had'em all piled up in a pyramid formation which make it just prime time for kids to play on'em. So, we played on'em.

There we were. Me, Timmy, Rosa and Huey, all out there playing cowboys and Indians. Well, true to his calling, Huey suggested we use the poles as horses. We started straddling them poles and commencin' to "yippy-ki-yayin'," and "giddy-upin'," and spurrin' them "horses" on.

I reckon you can picture in your mind what happened next. It turned out that the poles weren't stacked all together right. They started to move. Before we knew it, they were moving a lot. Me, Rosa, and Huey, all jumped off safely. But Timmy didn't. In all of the rolling of them poles, Timmy fell off and one of them rolled over his head. Well, me and Rosa started trying to get Timmy to wake up. We was crying so hard though, we was hardly able to do anything right. Rosa screamed at Huey to run to our house and get Mama. She called the police, who called for an ambulance. Well, they took him to the hospital where he was tended to for days and days.

After what seemed like forever, he finally came home. Everybody was gathered around him and crying and laughing and was so happy to have him home. People came by the house and brought cards and flowers and gifts for him. It was all about him and it was starting to get to be a little much. I mean, he was getting all this attention and I, the baby, uh, the youngest, was not getting any attention at all. Well, not to speak of, that is. I started thinking about looking for something for me to fall off of.

I heard that! Who said that? No, I am not being self-ish and stop saying that!

Well anyway, one of the presents Timmy got was a giant lollypop. I mean, it was gigantic, and because of the injury, Timmy was not able to open his mouth for a long time. That lollypop lay on that icebox shelf forever. FOREVER! Me and Huey would stand there with the icebox door open and just look at that lollypop, and look at that lollypop, and look at that lollypop.

Finally, it got to be too much. Huey said, "It won't hurt if we just take a lick, will it? That's all. Just a lick. Let's just take it out and take a couple of licks, wrap it back up, and put it back in there. Nobody will ever know".

Now I want to say it right out. IT WAS NOT MY FAULT? IT WAS HUEY'S FAULT!!

Anyway, I went in and got that lollypop, stuck it in my shirt, and we snuck down to the basement. Oh, that basement. The haven of havens. The shelter of shelters. The sanctuary of....oh! shut up, Kerry! Nobody would ever find us down here.

We got down there, and I took it out of my shirt, and we started licking on that lollypop and the more we licked the harder it was to stop. It coulda been dope 'cause there was no stopping us now. Before we knew it, it was all gone.

What were we going to do now?

"I've got it," said Huey. "We could say somebody broke in and robbed us."

"And they only got a lollypop?" I asked.

Well, what we finally did was, we took the wrapper and snuck back up to the kitchen and was about to put the wrapper back in. We had decided we would say it must have melted.

But then, all of a sudden, it seemed to get darker. There seemed to be a shadow looming over us, for right behind us, stood Mama.

Oh, no! Not Mama!

She grabbed me by the neck and Huey took off out the back door like a bat out'a hades.

(That was a word Mama would say 'cause we wasn't allowed to cuss.)

So, just like I told you before, it was all Huey's fault. But guess who got the whuppin'?

Chapter Eight

My
Big Brother

It took a while, but Timmy did get better, gradually. I was real glad. After all, he was my big brother. Even though he would give me a socking pretty often, he still kinda looked after me when he was of a mind to. Like one time when one of Junior's friends came over in this car his daddy bought for him.

The government had built this picnic area and wading pool over behind our house for the residents to bring their little ones to wade around in. There was also a gravel drive that went around the right side of our house and then into this area.

Junior's friend, Jerome was in the same grade as Junior, but a little older and, according to Jerome, his family was rich. He was always talking about them having all this money and going places and doing things that most of his classmates couldn't do.

Anyway, one day we heard all this weird sounding horn going off out back and we went out there and there sat Jerome in this old jalopy. He had drove all the

Him and Junior kept walking around the car, kicking the tires and hitting each other on the arm and laughing. They'd go back and forth putting one foot up on the bumper, saying a girl's name, then poking one another in the belly and laughing like monkeys. At this point I wasn't sure I wanted to get older.

Well, anyway, when he got ready to leave, he just jumped right in and drove on out.

So, I had the bright idea that I would help him and push his old car off. Well, I was holding on to the bumper when he started off and, in fear, my hands froze and I hung on pretty tight and Jerome started dragging me.

Timmy saw what was happening and ran real fast and caught up with Jerome and got him to stop just as he was about to get to the street.

Timmy ran back and saw me, still clinging to the bumper, with my bloody knees and feet. He started crying and grabbed me up and took me in to Mama. When Mama saw me, she started screaming and took me into their bathroom, took of my clothes, and put me in the bathtub. I felt kinda special 'cause I never got to be in their bathroom before. Timmy cried when I started screaming as Mama bathed me in alcohol. I mean, after all, he was my big brother.

Chapter Nine

Mama Had Her Times Too

Daddy seemed to be adjusting pretty well with his new job and all. That is as much as a kid can tell about what goes on with a working dad. Generally, all we knew was that he went to work, came home from work, and yelled a lot. Just kidding. He would come home and kiss Mama and then talk to us kids. Mostly he would talk to them about their school work and to me about if I had behaved myself that day. Go figure!

I did hear Daddy say he had some real good guys working for him that really cared about their work. He would get compliments from his boss also, so I think Daddy was real pleased with his situation. He knew it was because his men were doing their jobs real good.

It took him a couple of months to pay off that old car and trade it in for a nicer, later model, used car. He got a 1945 Plymouth sedan that had all the bells and whistles. A radio and a heater. It had nice seats too, that were not torn too much and a spare tire that even had air in it. It must have also had all the holes in the radiator plugged 'cause he didn't have to carry any jugs of water with him when he went somewhere. Daddy took a picture with Bertha Lou. I was so proud.

Jim Benjaminson's rare P-10 7 passenger

My daddy was a Christian man. Right after we moved to Childersburg he started taking us to the First Baptist Church. We went every Sunday that we were able. We had gone to church in Leeds, also. It was called a Primitive Baptist Church. They believed in feet washing and other rites that kept you humble. As I think about it, I believe we all could use more of that. But, we had to stop going there because Mama couldn't stop wiggling and giggling when she got her feet washed.

I remember one Sunday at the First Baptist Church, when the preacher was preaching on King Nebuchadnezzar in the Bible. You remember, the king had this dream and wanted somebody to tell him what it meant. Well, nobody could but Daniel. Daniel told him and he promoted Daniel to a high position. Then, after a few years, the king got all full of himself and thought he was as good as God. So, that was the end of the king.

It was a serious, quiet time while the preacher was talking about the king. The problem was, Mama was already knowledgeable about this part. When the preacher kept pronouncing the king's name as Nee-boch-a-razer over and over, Mama couldn't contain herself any longer. She, all of a sudden, tee-heed! out real loud. Well, Mama and everyone else in the church, including the preacher, looked directly at me. Now I ask you, WHY ME?

Daddy was so embarrassed he grabbed me by the neck (Any more of these neck grabbin's and people are going to start calling me Ichabod Crane.), and carried me out of the church, and I got a whuppin'.

When we got home, Mama confessed that it was her that did it. She told me she was sorry and I could hit her, if I wanted to. Of course, I didn't. We was taught to never, under any circumstances, could we hit a female.

Mama had her world, of course. ME! (Just kidding.) Thinking back on it though, I do imagine Mama had a time with me. Back in those days you didn't have to worry about all the perverts and kidnappers that you do today, so I had some lattitude, you might say. (Kinda like *The Little Rascals* did.) I was always getting into something.

Mama did have her friends in the neighborhood. Like Mrs. Cox, Huey's mama. I think she got me in about as much trouble as Huey did. But I couldn't hit her.

One time she saw me pulling up flowers in Ol' Lady Jones' flower bed, and called Mama. Mama was in the basement doing the wash. She'd got use to the wringer by then, but she told me one time that she never really got over that. She said every time she would start to stick something in that wringer, she would remember what happened that time.

Well anyway, she came running out the door and saw me coming. I knew Mrs. Cox had called her 'cause she said she was. She grabbed me by the neck and started dragging me home. I looked over and saw Mrs. Cox just a grinnin', but I was doing some hollering myself by this time.

After she drug me in the house, I told her, "But Mama, I was just pickin'em for you 'cause of all the hard work you was doing for us." Well, 'casue Mama was such what you would call 'a soft touch,' it worked. She let me go and told me to go play.

Then there was Mrs. Jones on the other side. She would invite Mama over for tea and just talk about what all they had and what we didn't have. Mama would come home every time upset about what all she said. But Mama kept going because she didn't want Mrs. Jones talking about her to the other neighbors. She probably did anyway.

Why, one time Mrs. Jones was telling Mama about somebody writing in chalk all over her beautiful stone walkway that led to her azalea garden. She said she knew who did it and was going to go right over there and tell Mrs. Cox. She said she saw Huey out there and he had something in his hand that looked very much like a piece of chalk, and he also had a handful of her azaleas. Mama knew who really did it, but she wasn't about to tell her.

Another time I went into the kitchen to get me some water, and there sat Mama at the table just a crying. I asked her what was wrong and it kinda startled her. She didn't know I was anywhere around. She jumped up and started looking around for something, and said there was nothing wrong she had just been slicing onions and the juice got in her eyes.

Funny thing was I didn't see any onions around, but I did hear one of her 'stories' on the kitchen radio and this lady was going on about her boyfriend being seen out with another woman. That woman was crying and carrying on something terrible, but I just knew it had nothing to do with Mama's onions.

You know, from walking around in the wading pool with my shoes on, to swinging my legs out the upstairs window, and pouring out Daddy's open oil cans in the driveway, I had a hard time finding anything to do.

One time I followed this little snake all over the middle of that cul-de-sac lawn, poking it with a stick. Every time I poked it, it would make this funny sound with its tail and try to bite me, but when Mama called me in to take my nap, I just let it go. I was going to tell her about it, but when I saw she had some chocolate milk with marshmellows in it, I forgot all about it.

When the others started to school it got real lonesome around there. They didn't have much time for me at all. From Bertha Lou and Lora Lee it was, "Did you see what Buddy Bimbaugh did to Piggy Davis today?" or, "Did you see that Bobby Hightower. He is the cutest thang." or, "I get so tired of doing math. That's all we do, math this and math that." Mama had to put up with this all evening long.

Chapter Ten

Not the Tennis Courts Again!

Junior was always on Daddy about driving. Because of Jerome, he wanted his own car so bad he could taste it. Daddy kept telling him we couldn't afford another car, but Junior just kep' on anyway. Daddy told him when he got his driver's license, he would let him drive.

A couple of days later Daddy started teaching him about how to start the car. Junior had a hard time remembering you had to mash in the clutch before stepping on the starter. The starter was a button on the floorboard. He would just hit that starter with his foot and the car would jump about ten feet and scare him, Daddy, and anybody else that happened to be close, near to death.

When Junior finally got that part down, Daddy showed him how to put it in neutral and then you could take your foot off the clutch and it would just sit there and idle. When he finally learned to do that right, Junior would sit there with the car idling, and just grin.

Next Daddy showed him how to put it in first gear and then mash the gas and let out the clutch real slow at the same time to get it to go. Junior practiced on that gear shifting stuff 'til he could do it in his sleep. (Or he thought he could.)

So, he told Daddy he was ready to give it a try.

That was when Daddy took him over to the new tennis courts to practice. (I thought, "Not the tennis courts again.")

One side of the courts was finished and one side didn't have any nets or net poles up at all. Daddy thought this would be a good safe place to start Junior out real slow. Junior got in the driver's seat and Daddy got in the other side. Now, just like all other kids for their first time, Junior was perfect. (Yeah, right!)

Daddy told him to mash in the clutch and put it in first gear. Junior mashed in the clutch and put it in first gear. Then Daddy told him to let the clutch out real slow and mash the gas just a little bit. Well, this is where it got kinda confusing with him having to do two things at one time. Junior mashed the gas alright, but he mashed it too hard. Then he let the clutch out alright, but he let it out all the way too fast.

Before Daddy could turn off the key, the car shot across that tennis court to the other side and knocked over the two iron posts holding the net. By that time, the net was all wrapped around the front axle and then he'd crashed into the high fence surrounding the courts and brought it all down. It was a sight to behold!

I reckon somebody musta called the police 'cause we heard this siren and right quick a police car came sliding right up there. When they got out, Chief "Pop" Minn just stood there with his hands on his big, fat hips and qawking all around.

Now, had you ever seen Chief 'Pop' Minn, then you would understand all of this. He was about five feet tall and weighed about three hundred pounds, and had no neck a'tall. He had his stupid deputy with him that was about six feet tall and weighed about a hundred and fifty pounds.

Well, the chief started waving his arms around and wanting to know who was going to pay for all of this. (That was always the first thing he said when anything happened because he was afraid he had done something wrong.)

After Daddy explained to him what all happened, the chief calmed down. Daddy told him that, on the good side, there wasn't nobody out there playing, so nobody got hurt. To which the chief told him he'd a been in a lot more trouble if that had happened.

Naturally there was a fine to be paid and the damage to the tennis court had to be paid also. Fortunately, we had car insurance that took care of the car. Daddy made Junior get a job working with the janitor after school and in the mornings. He also had to do odd jobs in the neighborhood till it was all paid back. Daddy helped out a lot though, by also making payments.

Junior was all talked out about driving the car, but it was quite the subject of conversation around the house for a good while. I didn't mind though, at least they weren't talking about me. I think we all steered clear of those tennis courts for while.

All I had was Huey, but most of the time I was mad at him for causing me to get whuppins'. I reckon I got a whuppin' 'bout one every two-three days, give or take a day or two.

Generally speaking, though, after a year, I think we had adjusted real good. Except for me and that toilet that is. Imagine, sitting right out there in the open like that. It just wasn't decent. What if......eeyuu. YUCK!!

Chapter Eleven

"Times they are a changing"
(Bob Dylan)

Well, I guess you can't expect things to stay the same forever. We'd been here about three years and had got to liking things the way they were.

Daddy liked his job. Junior liked getting to drive sometimes, even with Daddy hollering at him. Bertha Lou and Lora Lee liked boyfriends and movie stars.

Rosa Sharon liked school. Timothy Aaron liked riding the bus and I liked having everybody's attention. Mama liked the house, neighbors, and even the washing machine.

But, all good things must end sometime.

Only Daddy knew about when those things would end. He worked at a military defense ordnance plant and knew that when the war ended, the plant would eventually close. A lot of the workers there had mixed feelings about that.

They wanted desperately for the war to end, but at the same time they knew that it meant they would no longer have jobs. It was a little scary for some. Daddy tried to prepare us, but we didn't want to talk about it.

When the war ended, there was the biggest celebration the likes of which you've never seen before, or since, in Childersburg. There was, literally, dancing in the streets. Then another reality began to sink in.

Almost immediately orders came down from headquarters to start preparations to shut down the plant. It went on for, I don't know how long. Everyday you would see men, women, children, cars, trucks, wagons, and trailers all heading out of town, to where, most people didn't even know. Most of these people were a big part of the 20,000 or so labor force that had flooded the area, as soon as they could, for the jobs at the plant. They lived in tents, trailer parks, thrown together clapboard houses, abandoned shacks and boarding houses. I guess you could say that there are two sides to everything. The war ended (great). No more jobs (not so great).

Then, there were the managers, supervisors, office workers and such that also had to go. These were, perhaps, the higher paid people that maybe had particular places to go to, and some money to get there.

Daddy, you would say, came in that last group, but with a difference. Being the electrical supervisor, they had to keep him on longer to oversee the proper shutting down of the electrical operations. That was a pretty big responsibility. It gave us a little more time to make decisions about what to do next.

This was a confusing time for a young boy. I was just standing around watching everybody else running around and not knowing what was next.

There were two things (among many) weighing heavy on Daddy's mind. He was losing his job and the house we were living in was owned by the government. We would have to move.

So, while he's busy doing all the closing down of the electrical work, he was also trying to find another job and another place for us to live. Number two seemed to be the most difficult. He was pretty sure he would be able to find another job, but where to live was another thing. Childersburg still had a lot more people than homes.

Then, as always, God showed that He was still in control. There was a man on Daddy's electrical crew that owned a farm in Winterboro. Winterboro was about

10 miles west of Childersburg on Highway 76. The farm was about 1000 acres and he said he would allow us to live there if we could just look after it. He had worked for Daddy this whole time, and so he knew what kind of man Daddy was. Well, praise the Lord.

Way back in the late 18th century a poet named William Cowper wrote, "God moves in a mysterious way; His wonders to perform…." This was certainly an example of that.

Daddy came home and told us about this new development and there was a myriad of reactions at our house. Mama was okay with it but wanted to know about the house. Of course, Daddy couldn't tell her anything about the house except what Mr. Wallace had said. It was considerably smaller than our current house, but so was where we had come from.

Junior had just finished high school and was thinking about joining the army so he was fine with whatever. Bertha and Lora was really upset about leaving their friends and boyfriends, so they cried a lot. Timmy and Rosa fought all the time so they figured they could do that in Winterboro, just as well as in Childersburg.

That left me. I told them, "I am supposed to start school this fall and I'm already learning how to tie my shoes, and everything." I said, "Huey's mama has already bought his school supplies and clothes and we hadn't even bought mine yet. So, what about all that." Mama just looked at me and said, "None of that has anything to do with anything Kerry, so just shut up."

Chapter Twelve

Just Looking for a Home

Daddy told us that, come this next weekend, we would drive out there and look the place over. Then I heard him tell Mama, "It doesn't make much difference what it is like, we don't have any choice but to take it. We'll be living there practically rent free just to watch over it. There is a few cattle, but we don't have to take care of them."

"There is hay, but we don't have to cut it, or bale it, or put it up. Some one else will be doing that." So, we were all looking forward to riding out to the big city of Winterboro this Saturday.

You recall I mentioned earlier that Daddy was sure he would be able to find another job? Well, he had heard about a big plant that was being built a little farther down the road from AOW and he had already been planning to check it out. He talked to a couple of fellows at church about this plant. It was a national manufacturer of rayon cord used in the making of automobile tires. Daddy figured everybody needed an electrician. How right he was!

Daddy went down to the rayon plant after work the next day. He explained his situation and requested an application and interview for an electrician. He was given an appointment for one afternoon the next week. The secretary told him that since the plant was still being built, he may have to wait about a month or so, before they would be hiring.

When Daddy told us this at home, we were all disappointed. However, he said he felt pretty good about it for two reasons. First, he really didn't think the secretary was very knowledgeable concerning the employee issues. The other reason was because he believed the plant would probably need more electricians during the construction, and when bringing it online, than when it was already up and running. Naturally, I didn't know an elec from a trician, but to the men at church, it made a lot of sense.

Now, let me see if I've got this right. In a period of two weeks, we've gone from a job, to a no job, to a possible job, and from a house, to no house, to a house. Did you get all of that? Maybe you could explain it to me.

Childersburg went through a lot of changes during this time. It was different when the plant was being built. Back then people were coming in and things were looking real good. Money was flowing in from every direction, like sales for goods and services, sales taxes, schools and school teachers. It was a real boom time.

Now, things were not looking good and people were leaving in droves. The schools were in a big flux, so to speak. Fewer students meant less money, which meant fewer jobs for teachers, lunchroom staff, janitorial staff and all other needed supplies. The closing of the plant meant not only losing those jobs, but also many other jobs as well.

Most of these people were a big part of the 20,000 or so labor force that had flooded the area, as soon as they could, for the jobs at the plant. They lived in tents, trailer parks, thrown together clapboard houses, abandoned shacks and boarding houses. The available housing were still practically non-existent.

Then, before you knew it, it was Saturday morning and time to go look at our next home. We all piled in the car and took off. Daddy had a seating plan that put us all in our place.

Junior sat up front in the middle with Mama by the door. Normally, Junior would demand the "shotgun" position, but now he wanted to sit next to Daddy to be able to shift the gears. So that worked out good. That left the back seat. Bertha Lou sat by one door with me in her lap. Lora Lee sat by the other door with Rosa and Timmy in the middle. Boy, Daddy was going to get that job, for sure.

So off we went in the heat of a summer day, eight sweaty bodies and all four windows down. In the back seat we were singing anything that would come to mind. Sometimes we would all be singing the same song. We was as happy as pigs in slop.

Up front, they was singing a different tune. Junior was trying to change the gears with Daddy telling him where to put it. (Watch what your thinking there.) Junior would put it in third when he was supposed to put it in second, and then try to change it before Daddy could get the clutch mashed in. The gears would be grinding real loud and the whole time Daddy was hollering at him about not even knowing this part yet.

Now Mama, she was already crying from the time we came out the back door. She was having to give up her beautiful house, soap operas and tea in the afternoon, while Kerry took a nap upstairs (yeah, right). So, all the way there, Junior was trying to work the gears, Mama was crying, and Daddy was hollering at Junior and trying to console Mama at the same time. It was a real good ride.

On the way there, Mama had kinda quit crying, but was doing a lot of sniffling. But, when we turned off highway 76 on to a dirt road, Mama started crying again. Then, after about two miles of dirt road we turned into the dirt driveway. It was dirt in the front and dirt on the sides. Boy, you could have heard Mama in the next county.

You remember how we got out of the car when we first got to our house in Childersburg? Let me refresh your memory. "…we started climbing out of the car in slow motion like we was in a movie, all the while staring up at the house. We had never seen anything like this, except maybe in the movies or funny papers."

Well, it was the same thing here, except different. Real different!

Chapter Thirteen

It Ain't The Taj Mahal

At first look (second and third, too), the house was a big disappointment.

To start with, Mama wouldn't even get out. It took us a while, but we was finally able to coax her out, real gentle like, trying to stay out of her reach.

Now, let me describe the place as best I can put it into words. The yard was humongous, and all dirt. Did I say it was a lot of dirt? The house sat back about fifty feet from the road. There was a huge oak tree about halfway between the road and the house, with a limb just perfect for a rope swing. If we just had a rope.

Behind the house was a barn about twice the size of the house. It looked newer than the house. We would haveta' check that out later. Out to the right of the house (if you're facing the house), was a windmill. A windmill? What would we need a windmill for? Junior said it was probably just an old relic kept around for curiosity sake. Right?

Now for the house itself. Junior broke the silence with, "Well, it ain't exactly the Taj Mahal."

Daddy hit him. Mama started crying again.

The front porch looked like it would break down the next time someone stepped on it. But, as they say, "Looks can be deceiving." Because it was actually pretty sturdy and safe.

When you walked in the front door there was the livingroom/bedroom. One big room with a large, black, iron, potbellied, coal burning stove standing right in the center of the room. The stove pipe came out of the top and ran straight up into the ceiling and through the floor of the room above. It continued all the way up through the ceiling of that room and out the top of the house.

It was a unique way of heating an upstairs room without having to have a heater. As the stove got hot it would heat up that room and then, with the damper control, the heat, and smoke, would continue up the pipe to warm the upstairs. The pipe would be real hot, too hot to touch, and continue to carry the smoke and heat all the way up and out. The floor and the ceiling was protected from the heat by insulation around the pipe.

The stairs to the upper floor, was on the left of the door going into the kitchen.

The "living room area" was on the left side of the house, as you come in the front door. All the living room furniture would be on this side with the stove in the center. This would be the family room/entertainment center of the house.

On the right side was Mama and Daddy's bedroom. It looked like Mama was going to start crying again. Daddy said he would put up a curtain running from the front wall to the wall on the right side of the kitchen door for their privacy. As soon as he could, he would replace that curtain with a wall.

Continuing through the door to the kitchen, immediately on the right, there was a wash sink against the wall, with a window above it. The washing machine would be right beside the wash sink so it could drain into the sink.

Remember, the refrigerator, stove and washing machine came with the other house and we could not take them with us. Daddy said he wished we still had our old ones that the movers kept. Even the basement toilet had to stay there. (Thank the Good Lord.)

Then on the left of this area, right across from the wash sink, was the bathroom. It was very small. It had a lavatory, with cabinet and mirror above it, and a big bathtub (with rust) and a toilet. Daddy said he would put up a curtain in front of the tub. Bertha Lou and Lora Lee was giggling. I didn't get it.

The last room on the first floor was the eat-in kitchen. There was no door or wall separating the washroom and the kitchen. The back door was on the right just past the wash sink that led out to a porch that went all the way to the back corner of the house.

On the back wall of the kitchen, in the left corner, sat a huge black iron cooking stove with four large eyes and a warming area. It required coal or wood and the stove pipe went up through the ceiling, like the one in the living room. Mama wouldn't have any trouble learning this one. It was basically the same as the one she had in Leeds. She started to cry again. Oh, I forgot to mention, all of the floors were very clean, smooth wooden boards.

Chapter Fourteen

The Upstairs ain't no Boudoir

You remember, the stairs to the upper floor, was on the left of the door before going into the kitchen.

The upstairs, which was one big room, would be Bertha Lou's, Lora Lee's, Rosa Sharon's, and Timothy Aaron's bedrooms. I know! I know!

Bertha and Lora would have a full bed to share. Rosa and Timmy would each have a half bed. With the dressers and chest of drawers, everything would be placed accordingly, with Timmy's bed farther away from the others. Daddy said he would put up curtains just as soon as he could. Now, Bertha and Lora are starting to cry.

But, what about me and Junior? Well, if you went out on the back porch, to the end, you would see some stairs going up on the back side of the house, to another room up there. This was the only way to get to this room, and this was our bedroom. The back wall was the same wall that was on the right, at the top of the stairs inside.

It was one room, with slanted ceiling and only enough room for a full bed, and chest of drawers with mirror. Also, we had a small table with a basin and pitcher to wash our face and hands. It was heated by the pipe from the kitchen stove going up through the roof.

We both liked it, but for different reasons. Junior liked it because of the privacy. I liked it because it was exciting to go outside and up the stairs to your own room. This was adventure living! Of course, at the time, I wasn't thinking about going to bed in the dark. (That will be settled later.) But, it was no 'boodoor.'

This has become our new home. Like that ol' philosopher, Junior said, "Well, it ain't exactly the Taj Mahal."

Now, about that windmill. I think that "ol' philosopher" missed one again. The windmill was actually the only source of water to the house. As long as the wind blew, the windmill would turn and pump water into a tank sitting about eight feet off the ground right next to it. Gravity would bring the water into the house. You can always count on gravity, but what about the wind.

Lastly, I guess, was the barn. It was real big. At this time it was full of hay in the loft and all around. A lot of hay. (And that ain't no hay. Ugh! Sorry.)

There was a wire fence going from the corner of the barn to the right, with a gate about midway between the barn and the corner out by the road. The fence continued down parallel to the road for as far as you could see.

If you looked way off, you could see some cows out in the pasture. So, that was it. Our next home in about two to three weeks.

Chapter Fifteen

One Family, Eight Visions

Now, the ride going home. That was the longest and quietest 10 mile ride I have ever been on. She tried not to, but you could tell Mama cried the whole way.

Daddy talked as much as he could. He told her it wouldn't be too long. Just as soon as he could, he was going to be moving us back to Childersburg, after he got the job at Beaunit. Also, beginning next week, he would start building the wall, with a door, to their bedroom. After that, he would also build a wall to separate the girl's room from Timmy's. That would leave about a third of the space for a table or desk to do their homework on and and a table with a basin and pitcher for washing and other things.

That helped some with Mama's feelings, of course, but what he didn't remind her of was, that it would, in no way, be like the house on Pine Crest Drive.

Also, he would not be making as much money as he was now, and this house would not be entirely free.

During that drive home which, as I noted, took what seem like forever, everyone seemed lost in their own thoughts. Junior, who was planning on joining the army anyway, didn't mind the room upstairs too much, because he liked the privacy. He could practice his saluting and marching and waving at the girls without nobody watching. He thought that was pretty much all there was to being a soldier, that, and grabbing your gun and jumping on the truck.

Junior had grown up a lot in the last couple of years. He was now being more help to Daddy, what with him having his driver's license and all. He could do things and pick up things so Daddy wouldn't have to stop what he was doing.

I forgot to tell you about Junior getting his driver's license. Of course, it took place in Childersburg at the city hall. The officer was an Alabama Highway Patrol officer. Junior did real good on his writin' part and then had to wait about thirty minutes for his drivin' test.

The officer had been doing several drivin' test in a row without a break. By the time he got to Junior he was in a fix. He told Junior to drive over to the high-way to the Texaco station and stop there. After a little while, he came out of the restroom and told Junior to just drive back to the city hall. That was it! No parallel parking, no stopping at the stop signs, and no giving signals or backing up. Just drive to the gas station and sit. Boy, Junior was mad. He felt like he had done all that studying and practicing for nothing. Daddy had to calm him down and tell him how lucky he was. I don't think Daddy was too sure that Junior would pass.

Now, like I said, Junior was getting more mature and was helping the others with their homework and stopping fights when he could. He would help keep us out of Mama's hair whenever he could.

Oh, I have failed to mention that Junior was pretty smart, too. He always, even in the midst of his complaining and carrying on, brought home good grades, especially in math. I think he took after Daddy in that department.

After he and Daddy talked about it, Junior decided that he was not going to join the army. He knew The Army would be disappointed and all, what with him having all that practice. But, he could see that getting a job on the construction crew at this new plant might be best for everybody.

Daddy was pleased about that. He didn't say a whole lot about it, but he would of been worried about Junior being in the army. He knew, what with Junior still having trouble walking a straight line, he'd have trouble trying to march, and he didn't even drink.

Daddy never got drafted hisself, because of the size of his family. I think they kinda felt guilty about taking men with big families. Even so, he felt kinda guilty about it when it came up, among his friends. Unbeknownst to Mama, he had gone down to the army place one time in Leeds and tried to join, but they wouldn't take him because of that. Somehow Mama had found out about it, and she cried. I'm not sure if Daddy was sad or relieved, but after that, at least he was able to say he tried.

Bertha and Lora was kinda coming around to changing their tunes after Daddy said he would build 'em a wall. Now, they would have more room on the walls for all those movie star magazines and pictures they was planning to put up.

They also had their favorite boyfriend's school pictures, and movie star pictures, that they would look at, and giggle and take on about. They even talked about the new school they would be going to. Their room was going to be a real gooey mess if you ask me.

Rosa had mixed feelings about the whole thing. She already knew that Bertha and Lora considered her too young to include her in their "business." She also knew Timmy had his plans to collect snakes and frogs and other critters and bring them up there. So, she was real conflicted about this whole arrangement.

What she didn't know was that the girls had already been talking about spending more time with her and showing her all that girly stuff and teaching her how to put on make-up and such. I thought that was really good of them and she would be real tickled about it. I was pretty proud of 'em myself.

Now Mama! She was in a real pickle. She had to figure out how to move from a big house to a little house. What to throw out and what to keep. She knew she couldn't take the appliances but, where to get more was a mystery to her.

She knew Daddy was already doing some figuring on that, but what does a man know about what a woman needs, especially when it comes to appliances and such. Besides, he wouldn't even know what colors would go with the walls or what would match what with the other furniture. Men were just helpless when it came to things like that.

So, she cried a lot.

She wanted to go see each of her neighbors and tell them bye. That was important to Mama. It'd been good for her to meet out in the yards and just talk. She'd never had neighbors like that before. I mean, how many of us has ever had friends that would help you out with a little scamp like she had running around everywhere. She'd made some good friends there and she was going to miss them. She cried a lot during these last few weeks.

Well, if you think about it, all of us had things to do and think about, but it was nothing compared to what Daddy had to think about and do.

Chapter Sixteen

Good Byes are Hard

Sometimes it was like there was a mountain sitting on top of Daddy. He had his current job to complete, which was a real headache. Imagine having to shut down the electric grid of a huge plant like that and keep up with every piece of material and hardware in just three weeks. All the while having to follow government regulations on every step. It weren't no picnic.

Don't forget he was also having to give a lot of thought, as well as work, in the evenings and on weekends, to our new place. Sometimes he took Junior with him. He was planning the work and getting all the materials that he would need. He would be going out to Winterboro on the weekends and come home late. He told us they had a big general store there that had a lot of stuff he was going to use.

We would find out later that was a great store. It had just about everything a person could want or need. It had stuff for farmers and ranchers, and all your grocery needs. It said so, right there on the window.

Sometimes it's a lot harder being a daddy and husband, than holding down a job. Daddies have a lot on their minds. He really appreciated the help that Junior was giving too, carrying lumber and nails and tools and such.

Well, when that final Saturday arrived, and we were all ready to finish loading up the truck.......OH! I FORGOT TO TELL YOU!

Daddy's boss had signed a requisition for us to be able to use a truck to move. It turned out to be the same truck we had before. I figured they musta only had the one. I hoped they didn't need it before we got through with it though. I reckon they get a lot of use out them trucks.

Anyway, the man said we could use it as long as we stayed within a ten mile radius. I asked Daddy if we couldn't drive it more than ten miles, how were we going to get back from Winterboro. He told me that meant we couldn't drive it more than ten miles away. It was ok to drive it back. That fit in perfect. Daddy was so smart like that. He just patted me on the head and went on.

They couldn't give us any men to help us, so we would have to do it all ourselves. I figured those guys wanted to come, but they probably got tired just thinking about having to stop every few minutes to get water. You can't blame them.

Well, here we go! Daddy was driving the truck and Junior was driving the car. Me and Timmy was riding with Daddy and everybody else was riding in the car. Daddy figured me and Timmy would be too big a distraction for Junior.

As we pulled out around the circle people were standing in their yards waving and hollering. The ones that had not moved yet, that is. I'm sure you've probably already guessed it, Mama was crying and waving her hankie.

Mama cried a lot these days, but we all were hoping times would get better for her. We knew things would be hard on her, but she would have more of a purpose to keep her busy. She would be busy keeping the stove fired up, sweeping a lot, and teaching women stuff to the girls. You know, women's work.

(Uh, Oh! I've done it now. Please don't stop reading. I done gone too far into this thing for you to call it quits on me now.)

So, off we went on this ten mile trek to live in the country. As we were leaving Childersburg on Highway 76 and crossed over Tallaseehatchee Creek we were all kind of sad. But, on the other hand, we were excited about moving to a new place and having new friends. We didn't know there was nobody else living out there. It was a little hard, imagining friends, though. The last time we were here we didn't see anyone for miles around.

But remember, Daddy said when we were able, we would move back to Childersburg and our old friends. So, Winterboro, here we come.

Chapter Seventeen

From a Jack to a King

Daddy was a little quiet as we were going along toward Winterboro. Timmy and I were all excited and talking enough for three or four people, but when he said something, we shut up and listened.

He told us we were getting bigger now and needed to be more sensitive to Mama's needs. We should be helping her, as much as we could, with all the things she had to do.

He said a truck would be delivering coal to the house and pouring it into the big coal bin on the outside of the back wall of the kitchen. There was a bin door on the inside of the wall, near the stove. You could lift the bin door up, take the coal out and then either put it in the box beside the stove, or into the stove itself. We would also have to take it to the box beside the big heater in the living room.

Daddy told Timmy, that since he was the oldest, he could make a schedule for whose time it was to do the job. Timmy said we could check off the time when we did our turn. I was so proud of my big brother.

Mama was doing a lot of sniffling on the way to Winterboro, and it kind of increased a little bit as we turned off on to the dirt road. Then, a little bit more as we turned into the yard. You had to admit, it was different from the big house.

Something else was different, even from the last time we were here. The grass had been cut all around the house (Daddy and Junior did that).

The trash had been picked up all around the house and disposed of (Daddy and Junior did that). There were metal chairs on the front porch (Daddy did that).

The old mailbox was gone and replaced with a new one, post and all (Daddy did that). All in all, the first impression was a lot better.

But, it was still an old, dark brown, wooden house with very little personality to it at all. Junior helped Mama out of the car. We didn't know what to say to her any more. We'd said just about all there was to say. We were just hoping and praying Mama would last a couple of years here.

Daddy had backed the truck up to the front porch and pulled out a wooden board that was laying on the truck floor to use as a ramp. Daddy had gotten that board at the store in Winterboro. Daddy was so smart, he thought of everything.

We started to unload the truck while Mama just walked around in the yard looking all sad and everything.

Daddy winked at us and motioned for us to come into the house and through to the kitchen. Mama walked up the back steps and came in the back door and "screamed".

Us little ones in the back thought something bad had happened to her and we ran to the front of the others. There Mama stood in the middle of the kitchen.

She could not believe her eyes. Evidently, Daddy and Junior had really been doing a lot more work these three weeks that the rest of us knew anything about.

The kitchen was light blue with a yellow trim and the floor looked smooth and polished. The big coal burning stove was gone and a brand new General Electric stove was sitting in its place. Daddy had also bought a small coal-burning heater for the kitchen.

That's not all. The icebox was a brand-new, full-size Frigidaire with a little box-like freezer on the top shelf to make ice. It had a light in it so when you opened the door, you could see everything in it. Daddy said the light would go off when you closed the door, but I never could catch it doing that.

There was also a large wooden cabinet sitting beside the stove. Mama called it the Hoosier Cabinet. I didn't know who the Hoosier's were, but I hoped they wouldn't miss it. It even had a flour sifter in it. Mama was so happy that she just kept on hugging Daddy.

Oh, and there was a new washing machine between the door and the wash sink. The wringer then could swing right over the sink and the drain hose just

hooked over the edge of the sink. This was all a wonder to behold.

Even with all of these appliances and stuff, we still had room for the kitchen table and everything.

Daddy said he got all of these from Yarbrough Appliances in Childersburg. Mr. Yarbrough went to church with us, and he told Daddy he would sell these to us on credit. He was a fine man.

With all of Daddy's electrical experience, he was able to put in plugs for the appliances and wall switches for the lights and everything. He even added a light over the lavatory in the bathroom.

Well now, Mama was in hog heaven. She couldn't wait to get started cooking and cleaning. After all, isn't that what women......uh, never mind. I've already stepped in that one time.

There we were, standing around oohing and awing and laughing and carrying on. Mama was crying and hugging Daddy, and everybody else too. Then we remembered we still had work to do.

Daddy figured we needed to take the upstairs furniture in first so we would not be falling all over the living room furniture getting it in. Daddy sure was smart like that.

We started with the beds and when Bertha and Lora got the first frame upstairs we heard them screaming. We just knew they had seen some critter or bug, or something, but we ran on up anyway.

Well, to everyone's surprise, there was two rooms up there instead of just one. Daddy and Junior had done it again. There was one room just for the girls that even had a wall and a door you could close. It was plenty big enough for all their furniture and stuff. The ceiling light was for their room. They were so happy.

Mine and Timmy's room was basically the rest of the upstairs. We had room for a bed and chest of drawers and a table for all of us to use for doing school-work or whatever. The table was against the wall on the right with a lamp.

Now of course, this meant that Junior had the outside room all to hisself now. He had no problem with that. He could now come and go all he wanted, practice his saluting and waving at the girls, and not have to worry about kids getting in his business. Like we ever did, right?

There is one thing you could say for sure. Daddy had moved from a "Jack to a King" in one day, and once again, we could see that proverbial "cotton" getting higher and higher.

Winterboro, ready or not, we're here!

Chapter Eighteen

Settling In

It didn't take long for us to figure things out and get settled into each of our niches, so to speak.

Daddy, of course, went off to work every day. He and Mama would get up before daylight and she would, as quietly as possible, go up and get Bertha and Lora and somebody would ring for Junior to get up.

Daddy had rigged a cord up through the ceiling in the kitchen connected to a bell in case we ever needed Junior to come down (or wake up). He had also split off the pipe coming out of the water heater so Junior could have hot water up there.

Anyway, back to breakfast, they fixed just about the same thing every morning with only a little difference here and there. There was always plenty of coffee for them that wanted it and milk for us kids. We would have eggs, bacon or sausage, grits, oatmeal or cereal. It was pretty much whatever they was of a mind to fix, but it was always good.

Then Daddy and Junior was off to work.

Oh me! Did I not tell you that Junior had gotten a job on the construction crew at the same plant? I'm sorry. Sometimes I get to going on and on and forget what I've already said. Do you ever do that? I guess you've already noticed that about me.

But yeah, he went to work with Daddy one Friday morning when they were coming out here a lot. They decided he would just go ahead and apply. If not, he would have had to wait around the car all day, or Daddy would have had to drive back by the house and pick him up.

For the rest of us, it was pretty much the same every day. Mama, Bertha, and Lora would clean up the kitchen and wash dishes, and Mama would start the washing machine and do the ironing. Mama wouldn't let them do the washing yet because of what happened the first time she used the wringer.

When the clothes came out of the wringer into the sink Bertha or Lora would take the basket and hang the clothes on the line in the back yard. Mama didn't like for them both to do it together. A lot of the time they would get into a fight over who got what piece first. There would be water all over the place and the clothes would then have to be washed again. Sometimes it would get so bad that they would have to be washed themselves.

Rosa got to be the one to sweep and clean up the living room, and the girl's part of the upstairs. She always complained that she had the biggest job, but really, she just took longer to do it because she got distracted so easily. She always liked to sit and look at the older girl's magazines and their other things.

That left Timmy to clean up our part of the upstairs. All he had to do was sweep, make up, or change, our bed, and take our dirty clothes down to the hamper. To hear him tell it, you'd think he was being tortured.

Now, that was about it, and it was a fun time.

What? What do you mean, "What about me?"

Hey, I was the little one, remember? I had the task of helping everyone else do their jobs. If Timmy didn't do a good job, I'd tell on him. If Rosa sat around snooping through Bertha's or Lora's things, I'd tell on her. If Bertha had more to do than Lora, I'd tell her. I felt like it was my job to keep everybody else in line. I'll never understand why I was so mistreated as a young boy.

After our chores were done, we had pretty much the whole afternoon to do whatever we wanted.

Mama had what she called 'her stories' (soap operas) on the radio, and her *Kerry Drake* comic books. Yes, she still read these comics every time she found one.

While living in Childersburg and then Winterboro, every time anyone was going to the store, she reminded them to look for them. Daddy figured, being that she worked so hard, she was allowed at least one luxury.

Bertha and Lora, and sometimes Rosa, had their girly business with dresses, magazines, fixing each other's hair and talking about what the new school might be like. We only had two more months.

Chapter Nineteen

Saturday go to Town

Now, Saturday was a little bit different. This was grocery buying day and it was a really, busy day for Mama and Daddy, and usually took about a good part of the afternoon.

It was also an especially favorite time for all of us. During the week Mama would be making two lists for all the things we would need from the grocery store in Winterboro, and then from Childersburg.

There was usually a big rŏw over which of us was going to go. Naturally this was always decided by Mama or Daddy. Bertha or Lora usually had to stay home and do whatever housework needed doing, and me and Timmy got to go depending on how good Mama was feeling at the time.

Either Daddy or Junior would drive, depending on what work needed to be done, or repaired around the house. (Sometimes Daddy would think up things he needed to get done that, for some reason, didn't seem to get done by the time we got back.) If he needed something, he would just add it to one of Mama's lists.

The reason I said that me and Timmy got to go depended on how Mama felt, was that, for some reason, when we got to go, we would have 'accidents.' One time at the grocery store in Winterboro we was wandering around just looking at things and I found a rubber snake in one of the bins. I didn't know Timmy would go crazy when I poked it in his face. But, he did!

He hollered, jumped back, and knocked a big 'ol rack of fishing lures right over into a tank of live minnows.

Well, that caused the biggest hul-a-ba-loo you ever saw in your life. Mr. Matson let out a "whoop", ran over and was trying to scoop out the minnows into a bucket as fast as he could with out them getting snagged on the lures. Mama had to put the things down that she had picked out and just ushered us out hollering that Daddy would be back to set things right.

Daddy had to wait 'til the next payday to do it. We didn't get that long to get our 'payday.'

Then there was this time in Childersburg that you might say was 'memorable.' Mama loved to go to Moody Brother's Grocery Store. (That was right next to Sam's Pool Hall that I would become intimately acquainted with in the years to come.) Mama always liked going to the QuikChek grocery store for most things, but she much preferred the meats from Moody's.

Well, one time when Daddy came with us, we was in Moody's and Mama was at the meat counter in the back and Daddy was up front talking to Mr. Moody.

Me and Timmy was just wandering around minding our own business, when we saw these shelves with toys on them. You didn't normally expect to see this in Moody's, so we thought we'd take a look. Timmy picked up this little airplane, made of some light-weight something, with a hook on the front end and a rub-ber band.

There was nothing else to do, but for Timmy to put the rubber band on that hook, stretch it out and let go of the airplane. Well, that airplane took off, right straight for the front door. Now, how could anybody have known that the chief of police would walk right in that door at that time?

If you remember Chief 'Pop' Minn, then you understand all of this. He was about five feet tall and weighed about three hundred pounds, and that airplane hit him right in that area where a neck was supposed to be. He gave out the loudest holler, his feet went up, and he went down like a hunderd pound sack of taters. He went all purple and we thought he was dead.

Everybody ran to him but, was afraid to touch him for fear he would pop. Finally, 'cause he was sounding like he couldn't breathe, Mr. Moody thought he would try to unfasten his gun belt. He wasn't sure where to start though because, since he was so big, his gun belt was two gun belts fastened together, but with one buckle and one holster.

Anyway, he finally got his belt loose and the chief started breathing better and was able to talk. The first thing he wanted to know was, "Who hit me?"

Nobody really knew what caused him to fall ('cept us, that is), but everybody saw the mess. When he fell, his feet hit this large display of flower and vegetable seeds and they went all over the floor. Right on top of the pile was this paper mache airplane.

When Daddy looked at Timmy and saw the rubber band in his hand, he knew exactly what happened. Daddy immediately started helping the chief up and telling him he just slipped on something and would be alright in a minute.

Mama came up from the back and asked Daddy what happened. He looked at her, then looked at Timmy and said we needed to go. Mama paid for her meats and we left.

This time it was Timmy that got the "whuppin'".

Chapter Twenty

Radio Magic

Now, nights at the old homestead was a different time entire. Every weeknight we would gather around the radio in the living room and listen to our favorite shows. Televisions had barely been invented and nobody had one except them people in big mansions. But, between you and me, I think it was always better when you were able to use your own thinking than being told what to think. But that's just me.

Mama and Daddy always got the couch with whichever girl beat the others to it. The other girls got the chairs, with the floor rugs being for me and Timmy. We didn't mind that 'cause we could just waller around all over the floor. This was the best of times when you could listen to all sorts of shows and bring them to life in your head, which I was very good at.

Every night they was different ones. There was the scary or suspenseful shows like "The Creakin' Door", "The Whistler", "Sam Spade", "Richard Diamond", "The Shadow Knows", "Dragnet", "Boston Blackie", and

"Johnny Dollar." When these shows was on, I tried to sit a little closer to Daddy's feet.

Then there was the funny shows like, "Fibber McGee and Molly", "Amos and Andy", "Jack Benny", "Our Miss Brooks", "Ozzy and Harriet", "Archie Andrews", "Baby Snookums", "Blondie and Dagwood" and, "Dean Martin and Jerry Lewis." I didn't always get it, but I just laughed anyway when everybody else did.

Also, there was the live variety shows like, "Bing Crosby", Perry Como", "Bob Hope", "Danny Kaye", "Kate Smith", "Dinah Shore." These singing ones I didn't care too much for. I already knew how to sing.

What would really bother me was, when on one of them serious shows somebody would, all of a sudden, break out in song. That would just ruin the whole plot. You wouldn't ever see Kerry Drake start singing while he was in a fight with Two-gun Millie.

Saturday mornings were the best for us kids, though. There was, "Gene Autry and Champ", "Roy Rogers and Trigger", "Charlie Chan" (He was a Chinaman), "Superman", "Batman and Robin", "Buck Rogers", "The Cisco Kid and Pancho", "Rex Allen and Koko", "The Lone Ranger and Tonto", "Dick Tracy", and Mama's favorite, "Kerry Drake."

It was different ones at different times. These were all real good. I didn't care which one came on next, I liked them all. Radio time was a good time. Sometimes scary and sometimes funny, but all times memorable for bringing us all together.

Chapter Twenty-One

Sunday go to Meeting

Remember I told you that Daddy made sure we was a church-goin' family? Well, starting with that first Sunday there, we went to the Winterboro Baptist Church.

To go to Winterboro from the house, you would go back down to the highway, and turn left for a couple of miles. Winterboro was just a "T" intersection with highway 76 ending on highway 21. When you got to the stop sign, the general store was directly in front.

The church was on the left across from the school. It was a nice church, and the preacher was Pastor Claxton. He and his wife lived right next to the church in a nice little white house. Mrs. Claxton was my Sunday School teacher. She was real nice. She read from this little book and talked about Jesus when He went out into the desert and fussed with the devil. That ol' devil was pretty stupid thinking he could trick Jesus. After all, He was God's son, and it don't get any better than that.

After Sunday School we all went into the big room and sung songs and stuff. The preacher talked about this guy named Elijah, and how he was a man just like anybody else. He told the king God wouldn't let it rain for three and a half years and then he let it rain. Boy, that'n really makes you think, don't it?

During the preaching hour, we got to sing real loud cause everybody else was singing. There was this older man up front there waving his hand around while everybody sang.

Timmy started waving his hand around and this big fat lady started looking at him real ugly. Daddy looked at Timmy and thumped him on the ear real hard. Timmy looked real hurt and almost cried, but he stopped waving his hand around. Just about then Mama smiled at us, so we just sang louder even though we didn't know any of the words.

After the preacher started preaching Timmy kept falling asleep. One time I kicked him in the leg, and he hollered real loud. Later folks said they thought he was getting in the Spirit. Me and Timmy didn't know what that meant, but we didn't argue about it. Howsomever, the preacher's wife did give us a great big smile, so we figured we musta done something good.

The preacher and her was standing at the door when everybody left, and she patted me on the head said she would see me at school. I didn't get it, so I just went on out. It was a nice service and they all welcomed us real nice. Did I say it was nice?

Back at home, me and Timmy would have the whole outdoors to play in. Sometimes we would play "flinch." That's where you take turns hitting the other on the shoulder and the first one to flinch loses. But, our favorite, and only, toy was the barrel hoop and stick. We played with that thing 'bout all day long. We got to where we could go from the house all the way to the road without losing the hoop. We figured that someday it would be in the 'limpics and we would both win medals. We practiced how we would walk around with all them medals on our chests.

But, after a while it got kinda boring and we would walk around looking for something else to do. One day we really went off the deep end, so to speak.

We was sitting around trying to think of something new to do and Timmy said, "Hey! Why don't we sneak one of Daddy's cigarettes and go up in the loft of the barn and smoke it." Now that sounded like a great idea. I was so proud of him. I could always count on him to come up with the best ideas. We'd seen Daddy smoke enough so that we figured we could do it too. Now, think about it. Boys, barn, hay loft, matches. Boy, the Lord was watching over us, huh?

But alas! After we'd done this a few times, one day Daddy had to go out to the barn. Well, we all heard the loudest manly scream you have ever heard. Of course, we all went running.

But when we saw Daddy at the door of the barn, holding burnt matches and cigarette butts, and staring at us, we started to back up and run.

Daddy, knocking down Junior before he could get out of the way, was on top of us so fast you would have thought he was shot out of a gun. We thought he would never stop whipping us. He would go from me to Timmy and back me and then to Timmy again and, well, you get the picture. He took the ashes, butts, matches and all the dirt and straw around them and put it all in our bed and made us sleep with that mess. We were not allowed to change the bed clothes for at least a week. After a couple of days, Timmy got the idea that he would hold up one side of the sheet and I would hold up the other side, we could shake most all of that mess into the middle. Then we could sleep on each side away from it. I wish I could say we didn't smoke again but, at least we didn't smoke again for a long time.

After a while, Daddy had got to feeling guilty about our whippins'. I think it was because Mama kept reminding him that, after-all, it was his cigarettes. So, he came home from work one day with a brand new, bicycle!!! We were so surprised 'cause we'd been trying to steer clear of him. Well, it wasn't exactly "brand new," but it was almost new and a great one. It was a girl's bike, but that was ok because we didn't know the difference anyway. It was rusty black, with no fenders and a rusty black metal seat. A real beaut, and it was all ours.

Now seeing as how we had never had a bicycle, or even ridden a bicycle, we were going to have what one might call a 'learning curve'. Daddy showed us how one would get on, and the other would push. It took a while, me being the slowest to learn, but after a few cuts and bruises, we finally got to where we could ride it pretty good. It was a whole new life for us. Now we could go farther up the road and back without anyone knowing we were gone. Who could find fault with that?

It was the riding up and down the road that we found out we had neighbors. Neighbors that we'd never seen before. It opened up a whole new world for us.

Chapter Twenty-Two

The Neighbors

One day when I was out riding by myself, like always I was about to turn left, but then I stopped. We'd always been going out of the driveway and turning left toward the main highway, then riding a little ways up and turning around and coming back.

However, this time I got a strange urge to go the other way. So, after standing there a little while pondering over this life changing direction, I decided I was going to go to the right. I don't know why, I just did. So, off I went in search of fame, fortune, and adventure.

I had only gone a little ways, and all of a sudden, I came upon a house sitting back off the road a piece. It wasn't even half as far from our house as the highway was in the other direction. I stopped and looked. Right here, so close to our house, was another house. It wasn't near as nice as our house, and you couldn't call our house "nice." In fact, what it was, was kinda rundown.

As I looked, I knew people lived there, 'cause I could see smoke coming out of the chimney and there was clothes on the clothesline.

As I continued to look around, all-of-a-sudden, I saw someone on the end of the porch. It was a boy! A boy about my age.

He had to have been there all along, but I had not seen him. We just kinda looked at one another for awhile and then, at the same time, we both smiled and waved.

He came down off the porch and I just dropped my bike and walked into the yard.

He said, "Hi," and I said, "Hi." He said, "My name is, Isaiah, like in the Bible." I said, "My name is Kerry, like *Kerry Drake* in the funny papers." We both laughed about that.

Then he said he knew who *Kerry Drake* was 'cause his mama read about him in the funny papers all the time. I said, "My mama does too," and we both laughed about that, too.

Along about that time, a lady came out the door and said, "Well, what do we have here?" Isaiah told her my name and we went through all that again and just laughed all over again.

She said their last name was Thomas and they worked this farm for the same man who owned our place. We thought that was pretty neat.

They said they had been living there about four years and had been getting along pretty well. She said her name was Ruth, and her husband Isaac, was out in the field along with their daughter, Mary. I told her all about us, more than she wanted to know, probably.

Now, back at home, Timmy had come out looking for me. First, he looked up the road, the way we usually went, and then turned and saw our bike down the road. He came running down thinking I might have wrecked or something. When he got down there, he came up in the yard and I told them who he was, and we all talked a while longer.

After a little bit, we heard Mama calling us. Timmy had forgotten to tell me that Mama had sent him to get me to come in for dinner. We all said we were glad to meet each other and looked forward to our whole families getting together and off we went.

When we got home, we were so excited to tell Mama about our new neighbors. We told her their names and that we had somebody to play with and Rosa would have somebody to play with about her age. Also, that the same man who owned our place, owned their place.

Mama was excited too, 'cause she figured she would have a lady friend to visit and talk with. So, after dinner, me, Timmy, Rosa, and Mama all walked back down to the Thomas' place. Mr. Thomas and Mary had come back from working in the field and they were all sitting on the porch.

Well, when Mama saw them sitting there, she stopped and said, "Why didn't yall tell me they were colored."

Timmy and I looked at each other and I said, "I don't know. We didn't think about it."

Mama just stood there for a minute and finally said, "Well, I won't either," and walked right up on the porch. We all just sat and talked just like we had known each other for years. Mama and Mrs. Thomas talked about canning, gardening, cooking, and a whole bunch of other things. But mostly they talked about Kerry Drake, his wife Sandy, Bottleneck, Dr. Prey, Mother Whistler, No Face, and other villains in the comic strip. They had a time. Mr. Thomas just sat, rocked, and laughed at them.

Me, Timmy, and Isaiah ran and played, rode the bike and played "flinch." Meanwhile Rosa and Mary talked about girl stuff, you know how it is.

When it came time to leave, Mama and Mrs. Thomas said they would get together real soon. Mama told Mr. Thomas she would tell Daddy about him, and they could get together real soon, also. We were going to like them a lot.

When we got home, I asked Mama why she stopped like that when she saw them on the porch. She said that you just have to be careful when you are meeting new people, but that she was real glad we had met them.

When Daddy got home we all told him about the new neighbors we had met. He said he was real anxious to meet them so, after supper that evening me and Daddy walked down for him to meet the Thomases. I wouldn't say he didn't trust Mama or us, it was just that he figured that sometimes women and children were a little too trusting. So, off we went down to the Thomases.

When we walked into the yard, they were all on the front porch. Mr. Thomas got up and greeted Daddy and offered his hand, which Daddy was glad to shake. They sat down to talk, and Mrs. Thomas brought out some tea and Daddy thanked her. They talked for a good while about all kinds of things.

They talked about our two lands that we lived on. They had been on theirs for about four or five years and was real please about how things were going. They got to keep all the produce they needed for themselves and also got to make good money from the sale of the rest. Like us, they were just supposed to take good care of the land.

After a little while, me and Isaiah got tired of listening to them talk, so we got up and walked to the back where Mr. Thomas had put them up a swing off a big tree limb. We took turns pushing each other and then went down to this little stream and floated some sticks pretending they were boats.

When I heard Daddy calling me, I went back around front, and he said we was ready to go home. They both said our families should get together and do something sometime. We went on home thinking this was a good thing and liking our new neighbors.

I think both families benefitted from this relationship. The mama's got to have someone of their own to gossip, ur, I mean, talk with. The daddy's had man stuff to discuss, like car repairs and fishing. Mr. Thomas would come up and help Daddy work on the car, and Daddy would go down and help him fix his pump on the windmill. It was just a good thing for everybody.

Chapter Twenty-Three

The Rolling Store

About every three to four weeks the most fascinating thing would happen. First, if you were out in the yard, you would hear all of this jingling and jangling and a loud motor coming up the road. After the first couple of times, you got to knowing what it was a comin'.

It was a "rolling store." We'd never heard of a 'rolling store" before. A big old, truck that was so loaded down that, sometimes you couldn't tell the front from the back. It had wooden sides and a big canvas that covered the back and sides and would roll up. It had all kinds of house goods and everyday utensils just hanging all over the outside.

The inside was a gold mine of possibilities and treasures. It had an aisle down the middle and had everything from farm tools to work clothes, sewing needs to shoes and work clothes. It had car tires and batteries and jacks. Just about everything you could think of. Best of all, it had candy and toys.

It was an absolute joy to see that truck coming up the road and naturally a boy of my intellect found it personally inviting.

I was driven by a man named, Mr. Wilson. He was about as old as the truck, or older. He said he and his wife used to own a store together but she died and he just couldn't stand to be there without her. So, he just piled all of their stuff on his old truck and started driving all over and selling stuff off his truck. He said it has turned out to be better than just sitting around and waiting for someone to come in.

One time when Mama and Mr. Wilson was looking through his "sewing-do-dads" bin, I had innocently(?) climbed up into the back of the truck and found a nice lollypop. Well after all, he had plenty and wouldn't miss this one, so I sat down in the middle of the aisle and proceeded to lick away. You'll never guess what happened next.

Mama and Mr. Wilson had found whatever it was they was looking for, so he got back into his truck and took off with me just a hollering like crazy. Unfortunately, this truck made such a terrible noise, what with having no muffler, and the rattling of all the stuff on the sides, and the tailgate being up, they couldn't hear me.

After Mr. Wilson left, Timmy started looking around for me and thought maybe I had gone to the bathroom. He picked up the bicycle and started riding it around the yard until he got tired of that and went in to see what had my attention.

He looked all over the house and couldn't find me. He went out to the barn and still, no Kerry. He then figured I was hiding from him. We had done that a lot in the days prior to getting the bicycle. He looked everywhere he knew that I would be hiding. But still, no Kerry.

He started to worry and told Mama he couldn't find me. They looked everywhere again. Mama asked him when was the last time he had seen me. He thought a minute and said it was when the "rolling store" was here. Then, it hit Timmy. Kerry was on the "rolling store".

He screamed! Mama screamed! Rosa heard the commotion and even though she didn't know why, she screamed. Finally, Mama told Timmy to get on that bicycle and catch Mr. Wilson. Now, how in the world was he going to catch a truck on his bicycle? But he went at it just as fast as he could, anyway.

Fortunately, Mr. Wilson's truck would not go very fast for fear of damaging his stuff. Also, his next stop was the Jackson's that was two miles up on the right before you get back up on the main highway. When Mr. Wilson stopped and turned off the engine, he heard someone hollering. He looked all around but could not see anybody. He then walked around to the back of the truck and could tell it was coming from inside his truck. He quickly let down the tailgate and there I was, big as 'Ike', sitting there licking on that sucker, and happy as if I had good sense.

Mr. Wilson was flabberghasted! He started flailing his arms hollering and everything. He wanted to know what I was doing there and how I got there. I thought he was mad about the sucker so I told him Mama would pay for it. He said he didn't care about the sucker but, was afraid my mama would kill him for taking off with me.

He put me in the front seat and closed up his store again then started back toward our house. It wasn't long before he met Timmy on the bicycle who was stopped in the middle of the road, waving his arms and hollering to beat the band. I thought he was funny lookin'.

Mr. Wilson told him he had me up front and was going back to our house. He told Timmy to just go on home. Well, you know Timmy. He was so tired from all that fast riding that he just got behind the "rolling store" and grabbed on to the back corner and let Mr. Wilson pull him home. At least he did think to let go before Mama saw him, though. Mama woulda' killed him.

Mama was standing out in the road watchin' for us to come and when I got down she didn't know whether to knock me down or hug me. I sure was glad she chose to hug me. She told me to never do that again and I said I wouldn't. Then she knocked me down.

After all of that, it turned out to be a really fun day.

Chapter Twenty-Four

Junior's Girlfriend

As summer came on Junior started having those Army thoughts again. Sometimes you could hear him up there practicing his marching and jumping on the bed like it was a truck. He'd be hollering out orders, "yes-sirin', no-sirin'", and saluting like nobody's business. He stomped around in his galoshers like they was real army boots. Let me tell you, Mama didn't take to it too good.

She would poke the ceiling with a broom stick and pull that bell string and holler up at him about jumping on that bed and all. But he just kept doing it anyway. He had a big hankering about that army business and was grouching about not having no girls to wave at.

Daddy tried to tell him that was not what the army was all about, but Junior just kept on doing it. Can you imagine having a kid that never listens.

Junior did have him a girlfriend, though. Her name was Janet and she worked in the dispensary there at the plant. The dispensary was what they called their doctor's office. (I don't know why they couldn't say, "Dr's office." It didn't seem that hard to me.) He met

Janet when he had to go get a shot for cutting himself on a saw blade. I thought it was bad enough that he cut hisself but, he had to get a shot too. Grownups sure are a worrisome lot.

After that he started finding more excuses to go to the dispensary. It got so bad that his boss had to tell Daddy to remind him that he was still on probation.

Sometimes Daddy would let Junior use the car to take Janet to the movie house in Childersburg. The movie house was owned by the Jemison family. They were really nice people, and I didn't know it at this time, but I would someday be in the same class with their daughter.

Anyway, Junior talked about Janet all the time. "Janet said this, and Janet said that". Mama told Daddy she thought he was getting too serious. I didn't know what she meant by that, but it didn't sound good. I mean he didn't act like he had a fever or nothin', but sometimes he would walk around like he was in a trance.

Mama had a way of saying 'things were getting serious', but things always seemed kinda regular to me. You know what I mean? I guess I just didn't have anything to compare 'em to.

I didn't tell Mama about this, but Junior had said something about having an argument with Janet about him wanting to join the Army. She didn't want him to join because the army had another thing working up over in Asia or Korea or somewhere like that. She said she was scared for him. Junior would tell her, "Real men joined the army." I told him not to say that in front of Daddy.

Junior came down for breakfast one morning with a big black eye that was swollen shut. Everybody jumped up talking at one time, wanting to know what happened. Mama had a fit. She commenced to running around getting him some raw meat to put on it and everything. The girls were all squealing and asking him if he was taking up for Janet. Us boys were wanting to know who won and what the other guy looked like.

Daddy just sat there grinning and all calm and everything. Finally, he asked Junior if it was his stick of stove wood and his _____ business. (Only he didn't say blank.)

Mama screamed and slapped Daddy with a dish towel and said he could just leave the table. Daddy just laughed and took a drink of coffee. Junior, black eye and all, from then on, had a brand-new respect for Daddy. But we never did find out how Junior got that black eye.

Chapter Twenty-Five

A Real Cowboy

Hey, let me tell you about our cows. Well, they weren't really "our" cows. They belonged to the guy that owned the place.

But, did you know that, with all that hay in and around the barn, the smell of it was very attractive to the cows. Although they had all that grass, over all that much land, they would still come up to the fence all the time wanting some hay. Who could figure a cow? They'd just stand there bellerin' and bellerin' about that hay, so naturally we would fork out as much hay to em' as we could.

According to our agreement with the owner, we weren't responsible for feeding those cows, but Daddy couldn't stand hearing them cry like that all the time. I really didn't understand it either, 'cause like I said, they had all that grass out there in the field. Besides that, I'd heard Daddy say that a lot of that grass grew up to be hay. Cows are funny, you know that?

There was all kinds of cows out there. Big ones, little ones, black ones, and white ones. There was brown ones, spotted ones, and red ones with white faces, too.

There was one particular cow that started coming around all the time and acting real strange. It would stand off by itself, not wanting any hay or anything, but it would just be looking around at us and bellering and bellering. It sounded just like it was crying.

Daddy said he thought he might have an idea about what was wrong with her, so he went through the gate and started trying to follow the trail the cow had left. I asked if I could come with him and he said, "Ok, but be careful and do exactly what I tell you and watch where you step." I said, "Yes, sir."

We walked around trying to follow the trail she had left and after a while we came upon this little baby calf. Daddy said he didn't know why, but it looked like it had died when it was born. He sent me back for a shovel and we buried it right there.

Daddy said he had been thinking that she might have a calf somewhere that maybe had died not too long ago. He had noticed that she had an udder that was just full of milk. Well, we went back to the barn, and he petted her and talked to her and made up to her. He made her feel safe to his touch and then he started milking her. She would look around at Daddy and just moan softly like she was thanking him for taking care of her.

Well, she 'preciated that so much that she started coming around even after her milk was gone. She was so friendly and all and we decided we would name her Sue. I don't know why Sue, it just sounded right, that's all.

Before long, one of us, (I don't know who.) got the idea that wouldn't it be fun to ride her. Rosa and Timmy decided that since it was my idea, I could have the honor of being the first to ride Sue. Well, I wasn't too sure about this idea anymore, but they said I would be the cowboy on the ranch, and they would start calling me Rex after my favorite cowboy, *Rex Allen*. I asked if we could call Sue KoKo, after his horse, but they wouldn't go for that.

Anyway, we got this wooden box and put it right beside her and I, very slowly, climbed on. It was kinda scary at first, so I sat very still. Sue just looked around at me, but she stood very still, also.

Timmy went into the barn and got a rope and put it around her horns. When I got settled down, he started pulling her very gently and at first, she wouldn't move. He tried pulling her again and she took just one step. He waited a little to make sure she was feeling better about it and this time she just walked right with him.

Boy, I was so excited. Here I was riding a cow. Who'd a thunk it? After that, we just started taking turns. When we opened the gate and pulled her out Sue was real nice about it. We started walking Sue around in the yard and she didn't try to run away or nothing.

Rosa ran in and called everybody out to see me riding on Sue. They couldn't believe it. They all thought it was real funny, except Mama. She said, "Yall better not be tracking in nothing."

Chapter Twenty-Six

"Whatcha gonna do when the well runs dry, Honey?"

With all this roping and riding going on, a body just don't give any thought about the days of summer being at their longest and hottest.

You certainly don't give any thought to water, except to drink it. About all the grownups ever think about it is to drink, wash clothes, water the garden, cook with it, and bathe in it.

When it came us kids, all we ever thought about water was for the swimming hole, or to drink it. We never gave a thought about having to have water for those other things I just mentioned. (I sure didn't ever think about getting a bath anyway.)

But the one thing nobody ever thought about was, running out of water. How do you run out of water? You turn on the faucet, water comes out. Who runs out of water?

Well, we did. Can you believe it? We ran out of water.

It seems that while we was having such a good time, something else was going on behind our backs. With this hot, dry summer, there was practically no wind to speak of. Without wind, the windmill don't turn the pump. When the windmill don't turn the pump, the pump don't pump water up into the tank. When the tank

don't have water in it, you don't have water. Look at all that figuring I did. Who woulda thunk it?

Now this was a very serious thing. Daddy said he would have to put his thinking cap on for this one. I really didn't think he ever took it off myself. Afterall, Daddy was a thinker.

Anyway, he remembered seeing a well down on Mr. Jackson's place down where the road ends on the highway. (That's where I rode to on Mr. Wilson's truck. We never told Daddy about that cause we didn't won't to worry him too much.) It was a right purty, rock-walled well, right out there in front of the house with a little roof over it.

So, me and Daddy went right down there to Mr. Jackson's place to see him about some water. Problem was, all we had was a wash tub. Now, it was a big wash tub, but how far would a wash tub of water go?

The Jacksons were some really nice people. They were kinda old and their kids had done grown up and left. I kinda got the feeling they were lonesome 'cause they took to me right off. For some reason, not many people did that.

He and Mrs. Jackson walked us all around their house and showed us a bunch of stuff. They had this big chicken pen with a whole bunch of chickens, big and little, with two big ol' roosters that didn't get along with anybody, not even each other.

There was these little chicks running around everywhere and they were so cute. I asked Daddy if we could have some, but he said, "no 'cause we didn't have a place for them".

I told him they could sleep with me and Timmy, but he just looked at me real funny, and still said, "no." Mrs. Jackson just laughed and patted me on the head.

They also had a large pig pen with two big sows in it (they said a sow was a mama pig) and about ten or so baby pigs that ran around squealing and making all kinds of racket.

There was also some middle size pigs that Mr. Jackson said would be hanging in his smoke house before too long. He said they'd be mighty happy to give us one when the time came. Daddy said he sure did 'preciate that.

There was also a big pen with two huge boar hogs in it (they said a boar was a daddy pig). I learned more about pigs that day than if I'd been in school. The part I liked best was that they got to lay around in all that mud all day long and nobody cared. As hot as it was, they had the best of the situation.

Mr. Jackson said something about what a job it was keeping them boars off them sows. Him and Daddy just laughed and laughed about that, but I didn't get it.

Mr. Jackson told Daddy he could have four big metal milk cans full of good water right out of that well. He also told us we could come get some anytime we wanted. We didn't even have to ask first. I think they missed their kids so much they would even like seeing me and Timmy. We felt real good about not having to worry about running out of water any more.

I learned right then and there how really great it was to have, and to be, great neighbors. You never know when you are going to be needing some help, so you should always be ready to be a friend.

On the way home I asked Daddy what Mr. Jackson was talking about when he said he had to keep them boars off them sows. He kinda cleared his throat, hem-hawed a bit then said, "Sometimes them boars would be roughhousing around, like boys do, and fall on one of them sows and hurt her." Now, that made sense to me alright, cause me and Timmy would sometimes knock Rosa around when we was playing. But I still didn't understand why it was so funny.

Anyway, now we knew what we were going to do when the well runs dry, Honey.

Chapter Twenty-Seven

Junior shows Janet

In the succeeding days we had a lot of contact with the Thomases. Either Isaiah came up to our house, or I went down to theirs. At our house we had lots of stuff to do. One favorite thing was to play with, or ride, Sue. She seemed to like it as much as we did. But we could tell when she didn't want to play anymore.

She would just stand there and not move, sometimes shaking her head, no matter how much we pulled on her. I didn't understand why she didn't want to play anymore when we would be having so much fun. So, we would take the rope off and let her go. Sometimes, all she would do was go out there and stand by this big ol' bull. That just didn't seem like much fun to me.

Other times we would take turns riding the bike. Isaiah had never rode a bicycle before, but we taught him just like Daddy taught us.

He learned real fast but he said his mama was always wanting to know how he got all them cuts and scrapes and bruises. We always tried to cover them up with rags and tape and stuff, but she somehow figured it out anyway. She was real smart like Mama.

If we got real hot doing all that stuff, we could always run a ways down behind the barn and jump in the swimmin' hole. It weren't actually a swimmin' hole. I was just a waterin' hole for the cows, but it worked out real good for us. You just had to watch your step a lot, though. We always had a good time with Isaiah. He was a good friend.

Sometimes Mary would come up with him and she and Rosa would play dolls or something like that. She only had one doll and it was just kind of a rag doll. One time I saw Rosa give her one of her dolls and said she could keep it. I think Mary, for some reason, got something in her eye about that time and had to go in the bathroom to get it out. They was good friends.

Now, it was 'long about this time that Junior made the final decision to join the army. Janet had got real tired of hearing him tell her he was going to join, so she told him, "Well, just go ahead and join then." So he did.

When she found out he'd really joined, she just cried and cried and begged him to, "take it back." But, it was too late then. They won't let you do that. They take real dim view about those kind of things. They take their job real serious.

When Junior and Janet came to the house and told us all, she and Mama just sat down on the couch together and cried and cried. Naturally, when they started their crying, Bertha Lou, Lora Lee, and Rosa Sharon joined right in with their wailing. Me and Timmy just stood there watching and wondering if we should be crying it too. Daddy came in and hollered for everybody to, "shut up." So they did.

Daddy asked Junior when he was supposed to leave and Junior said, "Next Tuesday." Well, this was Wednesday so, depending on your perspective, it was either too soon, or we had plenty of time to get ready. The plan was for Junior to come back to the recruiters Monday and pick up his travel uniform and papers. Then Tuesday he would meet the bus on top of Tank Hill in Childersburg at 6:00am and go to Montgomery. From there he would go to Ft. Jackson South Carolina for his basic training. Tuesday would be here before we knew it.

It seemed like the rest of the week went by in slow motion. Everybody just sat around in their own little world, and nobody wanted to do anything. Every evening Junior would just drop Daddy off and take right off to see Janet. He wouldn't come home till real late.

I went down and told Isaiah and his family about Junior and they said they was real sorry. Mr. Thomas said to tell him that they would be praying for him and to remember to duck.

Everybody got up real early Tuesday morning when it was still dark. Junior had packed the night before and was ready to go. We all got our hugs and kisses and watched as Junior took his bags to the car. It was a sad sight.

Mama had fixed him a paper sack full of sandwiches and said she would write ever chance she got and for him to write her back. He said he would. Daddy told him to always remember to duck, and then laughed. That was what Mr. Thomas had told him and I still didn't get it.

As they were about to pull out, I ran out to the car and begged Daddy to let me go. He looked at Junior, who nodded, and he said, "Ok," so I piled in the back.

On the way to Childersburg, I laid down in the back-seat and they thought I had gone to sleep, but I was just listening. You could tell that if he could have, Junior would call all of this off and go back home. This was the most scared that I had ever seen him. I think just about then he was feeling like a little boy in a big man's world. Although he'd never been in the military, Daddy talked to Junior about how to act and all. Daddy had worked with a lot of ex-military men that had told him all about what goes on in the army. He said the most important thing was to keep his head down and don't volunteer anything. They talked about a lot of other stuff, too and every time Daddy would say something, Junior would say, "Yes, Sir." All that "big talk" was gone, and he was sniffing a lot.

We got to Childersburg about 5:45 and Daddy pulled to the side of Highway 280 on what was known as "Tank Hill." It was called that because there was a great big water tank up on top of the hill. I wondered what a whopper of a windmill they had to have to fill that tank up.

When the bus came up over the bridge, Daddy flashed his lights at it, and it pulled over. We all got out and Daddy helped Junior with his bags and stuff. They just looked at each other for a few seconds and then hugged a long time. They both cried.

The bus driver got out and looked at Junior's ticket, then opened the side of the bus. You would not believe that great big 'ol hole in the side of that bus. You never would have known it was there.

Well, he threw Junior's bags in there and then he and Junior got on the bus. If there was anything halfway good about it, it was that you could see a bunch of other sad looking soldier boys on that bus for Junior to ride with.

When we got back in the car we just sat there and watched the bus pull off. Daddy was very quiet and sad and not in any hurry to get going. I had a lot to say about all of this, but I figured I better wait awhile and let Daddy start talking first. You might say that I wasn't too prone to making good decisions, but I think that was one time I made a good'en.

On the way home Daddy pulled over on the side of the road and said he had to check something in the back. He opened the truck lid, stood there for a little bit, closed the lid, and got back in the car. I noticed he had his handkerchief in his hand. It was a real quiet time all the way home.

Chapter Twenty-Eight

Getting Ready for School #1
(The Good, ...)

After we got home from church the next Sunday, we was sitting around the table after Mama's fine dinner and talking about what all happened the week before (sadly), and then about the plans for this next week.

Oh! By the way, talking about Mama's fine dinner, you just don't see anything like it anymore, and it's a crying shame. Fried chicken, with the crust, cooked in real lard. Mashed taters fixed with real milk and real butter.

Speckled butter beans cooked with a ham bone that still had some meat on it. Fried green domaters, with the crust, cooked in the chicken grease, and fresh apple pie. You just don't get that kinda eaten' anymore. (Excuse me while I wipe this paper off.)

Anyway, we was all talking and Mama said, "Yall do know that school starts a week from Tuesday, right?" We all just sat there with our mouths open. Except for me, that is. I said, "Hey, do yall realize I'm about to start school and I don't know a thing. I'm just plumb ignernt. Don't I need to do something?"

For some reason everybody thought that was funny. That just made me feel even more ignernt. Mama told me not to panic. She said she was sure I would know just as much as the other kids in my class. I thought, "Boy, that sure is going to be one ignernt class."

Mama continued, saying how we would all have to go to "registration" on Thursday night. She said we would have to register in four different grades, so we would have to be there a while. She looked right at me and said, "We all have to be on our best behavior, or they might not let us go to school here. (Everybody, but me, knew they had to let us go to school, it was the law.)

She said she would register Kerry while Bertha Lou and Lora Lee were registering themselves, and then they could watch Kerry while she registered Rosa Sharon and Timothy Aaron. It all made sense to me. It was simple. It wasn't rocket surgery.

"But wait a minute," Bertha Lou said. "What about Daddy? What's he going to be doing all this time? Couldn't Kerry just stay with him?" Mama just rolled her eyes to the ceiling and said he would probably be outside with the other men smoking, coughing, scratching and talking about how hard they worked today.

Besides, I don't want to have to go looking for Kerry when it came his turn."

Of course, we would all need new clothes of one sort or another to start school in. I knew I needed some shoes for sure. Daddy had already made me some new bottoms to my shoes this year, but even those were 'bout worn out. I tended to wear holes in the bottoms of my shoes faster than everybody else in the family.

I don't know why, but I would wear 'em right through everything I came to, water, mud, cow mess. Mama was all the time asking me why I couldn't stop walking in the mud holes and other messes. I told her I didn't mean to forget, but it would just happen.

When Daddy would make me some new shoe bottoms, he would take a big piece of cardboard and put my foot on it. He would then take a pencil and draw all the way around my foot on that cardboard.

Then he would take a pair of scissors and cut along the lines, and then, shazam! He'd have the whole bottom of my foot right there on that cardboard. It was a sight to behold.

Well, then he would do all of that all over again for the other foot. Next, he would take those bottoms and put them into my shoes, and I'd have a brand-new pair of shoes. Wow! Was my daddy smart, or what?

Anyway, back to Mama. She said she had a big surprise for all of us. She said ever since we'd moved here, she had been taking a little money every week from her budget and putting it aside for our school needs. Early in the year she had gotten ahold of a Spiegel Catalog. Well, we had no idea what a Spiegel Catalog was, but Daddy looked like he was well aware of what it was, and about now he was starting to get a little nervous about this whole thing.

But Mama had a head of steam going and was not paying no attention to Daddy. She said she had been getting some things every week in the mail when he was at work.

She had school dresses for all the girls with church shoes, and tennis shoes with peddle-pushers for their school play times. She had overalls, black hightop Keds, and brogans for me and Timmy, and church shoes, too. Now Daddy, for a while anyway, won't be having to make new shoe bottoms for me.

Mama got us all different kinds of coats. The girls' jackets were thick cloth coats each of a different color, and we boys got brown corduroy jackets. They was real nice. Everybody also got some good toboggans that kinda matched our coats. Boy! I sure didn't know we was rich, but it looked a lot like it to me.

Daddy started to feeling a little better when she brought out some overalls and brogans for him also. It was just like Christmas all over again.

We didn't know how we was going to wait another whole week to put all of this on. So, we didn't even complain, much, when she said we would have to fix our own plates for supper. Boy! I sure didn't know we was rich.

Daddy said he also had a surprise for us. He told us he was going to build us a little shed for us to wait in for the school bus.

Wait! School bus! What school bus? I told 'em nobody had ever said anything about a school bus. Timmy said, "How did you think we was going to get to school? Dummy!" "I didn't know?" I said. I guess I just figured Daddy would take us. I had been more worried about what I was going to do when I got there, not "how" I got there.

So, this next week was all a big whirlwind. We were all excited. I couldn't wait till the next morning to go down and talk to Isaiah about all of this, and about starting school the next week.

Chapter Twenty-Nine

Getting Ready for School #2
(......, the Bad....)

Right after breakfast, Monday, I jumped on the bike and rode down to see Isaiah. When I got there, he was out on the front porch snapping beans with Mary. I jumped off the bike and ran up on the porch and just started talking to beat the band. I was telling them about our new clothes and the bus shed Daddy was going to build and how we would be riding the bus together, and everything.

Wait! They were not reacting the way I figured they would be. So, I went back over it all again and, this time I acted even more excited. Well, it still didn't seem to be working. Finally, Mary said they wouldn't be riding the bus with us. I asked if their daddy was going to take them, and she said, "No, it's because we go to a different school from the one you go to."

MAMA LOVED KERRY DRAKE

When I asked her where they went to school, she said they went to Alpine School. She said it was down our road in the other direction toward Alpine. I told her I didn't understand, and she said I should go ask my mama about it. I said, "Ok," and slowly went down the steps, got my bike and went home. I heard Mary say, "Don't cry, Isaiah. I told you this would happen."

I puzzled and puzzled about this in my mind as I walked, pushing my bike, all the way back. For some reason I didn't know why, I felt some water on my cheek. Mama said it might rain today.

When I got home, I started talking to Mama about it, but before I could get it all out, Mama said, "I'm real busy right now Kerry. You'll have to talk to your daddy about it when he gets home."

Well, this was still morning, so I had all day to ponder over this. I asked Bertha Lou and Lora Lee, but they said they were too busy fixin' their hair and trying on their new clothes, so they didn't have time to fool with me. "Wait till Daddy gets home and ask him about it."

So, then I went and told Rosa Sharon all about it and all she said was, "Grow up Kid, go on, you're bothering me. Talk to Daddy about it when he gets home." I was beginning to get real depressed.

So, that left Timmy. My wise big brother. My hero. My sidekick. My smokin' buddy. The one I could always count on to get me in, and out of, trouble. He said, "Look

Kerry, let me give you the benefit of all my years of experience and wisdom. (I was feeling better already.)

"Life," he said, "Is full of all kinds of roads. There's dirt roads and paved roads. Straight roads and crooked roads. Roads that go up hills and roads that go down hills."

"So, I'm goin' down a road?" I asked. He said, "No, no, no. That ain't it. That ain't it at all." I said, "Well, I still don't get it." Finally, he just said, "Look Kerry, why don't you just wait until Daddy gets home and talk to him about it?"

Boy, I'd never felt so enlightened in all my life.

Chapter Thirty

Getting Ready for School #3
(....and the Ugly)

Well, I had the rest of the morning, dinner time, and all afternoon to puzzle, ponder, wonder, and try to guess, how it was going to go when Daddy got home. I knew he would have the answers to my questions, after all he was the smartest man there was. (You notice I've tried to make that clear all along here.)

So, I just tried to stay busy till he got home. I did everything I could think of to do, to pass the time.

I walked around to the back yard and talked to Sue, but she wasn't wanting to talk about it. I think I woke her up. It was hard to tell but, she was real good about it, anyway. She would just nuzzle up against me with her nose and get snot all over my arm. She didn't mean to though, she was just glad to see me. I tried watching where I stepped, but I wasn't always successful.

Next, I went up in the loft of the barn and laid around up there for a while, chewing on wheat straws and thinking. I think I did so much thinking that day I was afraid I wouldn't have any thinking left for school. They say you really have to do a lot of thinking there. Maybe I need the practice.

I went over to the windmill and stalked around that thing for a while wondering how it worked. I finally decided that if I was supposed to know, God would tell me. (That was how the preacher answered some questions he didn't know the answer to.) But I wouldn't hearing Him say nothin'. Mama always did say I didn't listen too good.

Long about late afternoon, I got the idea that I could go up into Junior's old bedroom. You know, the one you got to by going up the back outside stairs. Well, this turned out to be an adventure all it's own. (All right, calm down, don't be so impatient. I had to do something till Daddy got home.)

So, I went up the stairs and went in. It was the biggest mess you ever saw in yore whole entire life. You could barely see the bed. Of course, all of Junior's belongings were up there. You know, like when you die, you can't take anything with you, well that goes for the army, too.

There was stuff like magazines about war, and army men, and girls in bathing suits that you almost couldn't see. There was his old galoshers that he jumped around on the bed, uh, I mean the truck in. I could still hear him up there doing all that. Hollering about shooting yer gun and saluting and all. Of course, he wasn't doing much pretending about now. It was all for real, now buddy.

I also found some old letters and cards he had got from Janet before he left. I started to read'em, but it was just old kissy stuff and not really worth the time.

Well, it must have been time for Daddy to get home, 'cause I could hear him downstairs. He would always come in and kiss Mama and seek out the rest of us.

He asked where Kerry was and Mama started talking real quiet, so I couldn't hear from up there. I guess she was letting him know I wanted to talk to him about something.

Chapter Thirty-One

The Hard Truth

About that time the back screen door slammed, and I heard him hollering for me, so I went down the stairs and he grabbed me up and hugged me like always.

"Kerry," he said, "Your mama said you had something you wanted to talk to me about."

I said, "Yes, sir."

"Sumpn' heavy?" he asked.

"It's preyin' on my mind, Daddy," I said.

"Ok, let's hear it, then," he said.

So, I started with when I went down to Isaiah's to tell'em about the stuff we got and the bus shed you was going to build for us all and how we would all be riding the bus together, and everything.

Then I told him about how they didn't act the way I figured they would. So then, I said how I went back over it all again and tried to act even more excited this time. It still didn't seem to be getting through to 'em.

I told him that was when Mary said they wouldn't be riding the bus with us. So, I asked if their daddy was going to take them. That was when she said, "No, it's because we go to a different school from the one you go to."

I told Daddy that I didn't understand why they went to a different school, when they lived right here. He said there was a reason, not a good reason, but a reason.

I told him I still didn't understand.

He said, "Son, this has been going on for a long, long time. Do you remember when we talked about what the preacher said about how God made the heavens and the earth, and everything in them?"

"Yes, sir."

"And you remember that God made the first man and the first woman?"

"Yes sir, Adam and Eve."

"He made them perfect, right?"

"Right."

"You remember, when we talked about it, what we said that meant?"

"That, if they wanted to, they could do everything good?"

"That's right Son. So, what happened next?"

"The devil tricked'em?"

"Right again. How did he trick'em?"

"He lied to them, and they believed him, right Daddy?"

"Right again, son. Before this, they had been perfect, and then they chose to believe the devil, instead of believing God. The sins of selfishness, (believing in themselves, and not God), and greed, (wanting to be equal with God), entered into the world and forever became part of the human race."

"But Daddy! What does that have to do with Isaiah not being able to go to school with me?"

"Ok, calm down. Be patient. I'm getting to it."

"From that sin, now being inside Adam and Eve, when they had children, sin automatically went right into them also." So now, sin has gone all the way down through the human race, to today."

"We still have a choice to do right, or not do right. But the sins of greed and selfishness have given a lot of us the excuse to choose ourselves and all who look like us, to be together, and not be with others who look different."

"So that's why Isaiah can't ride our bus?"

"I think you hit the nail on the head right there, son. Way back there, some people got to thinking that because someone looked different from them, they were not as good as them. Also, they didn't want them to become equal to them."

So, they wouldn't let them go to school, or ride the bus with them. As a result, they did not get as good an education, and so were told that they were not as smart as us. That resulted in them not being able to get the best jobs, thereby, keeping them down. All because of greedy and selfish people."

"But we don't want to be that way, right Daddy?"

"Right, son."

So, what do we do now, Daddy?"

"Well son, there's not a whole lot we can do now, but hopefully there'll come a day in the, not too distant, future when most people will understand that we should judge a person by what he does, not by the color of his skin. That's what President Lincoln was talking about when he quoted the Bible, "All men are created equal." There is also a young man named King teaching that same message to the world today.

But some people, because of the sins I mentioned, still fought against it. We must always try to treat other people the way we want to be treated. Remember "The Golden Rule." Until then, we should all hope and pray to that end."

'Bout then, Mama called us all in to supper and when we sat down to the table, Daddy prayed about all of this and told God that we would trust him to work all of this out in His time. Of course, it was easier for us, being on this side of the fence, so to speak, to pray that. I just hoped I would be able to see it through till then.

After supper I got back on my bike and rode down to Isaiah's house and they was all the porch shelling peas. It was a big job, shelling peas, and just like at our house, it took everybody doing it, or it would never get done.

I walked up on the porch and started shelling some in Isaiah's pan. Mr. Thomas said he was expecting me. I guessed that either Mary or Isaiah had told him about our little talk.

I told them, "My daddy talked to me when he got home, and it helped me to understand the situation as best I can. I don't know what else to say but, we love yall, and want you to be our friends forever."

Our daddy's could still work on our cars together and fix stuff. Our mama's could keep gossiping uh, I mean talking about their soap operas, and *Kerry Drake*, and cooking and cleaning, and how good all us kids are.

We can still play together and jump in mud puddles together, and ride ol' Sue together." (Uh, oh. I forgot I wern't supposed to tell about that in front of them so, when Mrs. Thomas looked at Isaiah real funny, I just went right on talking. That was one thing I was good at.)

I told Isaiah that maybe we could do our schoolwork together 'cause I knew I was going to need all the help I could get. They all laughed about that. I didn't know why, 'cause I was real nervous about it.

Can you believe all this happened in one day? Its three more days till registration. What could I possibly find to do till then?

Chapter Thirty-Two

School Registration
(Are they serious about this?)

Well, when Thursday finally came it rained all day. Registration was supposed to start at 6:00 and Daddy got home about 5:00. Mama had supper ready when he got there so we would not be late.

We all had on our new school clothes, and everybody was in the car waiting on me. I was having trouble tying my new shoes and when I finally got them tied, I ran out the back door. The rain had made the back steps slippery and I tripped and fell down the steps. Guess what? I landed right in the middle of a mud puddle. The only thing that saved me was, several days before, Mama had asked Daddy to fill it in.

So, we had several issues here. Everybody in the car was piling out and yelling at me. I was lying in the mud puddle crying. Mama was yelling at Daddy for not filling in the mud puddle. Then, Mama had to get out some old clothes for me to wear.

Now, I was crying because everybody else got to wear their new clothes. All the while Mama was still yelling at Daddy and Daddy was just standing around looking down at his shoes. I didn't know why, they looked alright to me. All and all, it was starting out to be a great evening.

Now the school was in like a horseshoe shape. If you looked at it from the back, on the left was the grammar school side. On the right was the high school side.

If you started in the grammar school side, the first grade was the first room on the right. The second grade was the second room, and the third and fourth grade rooms were next, all on the right. As you rounded the corner, the fifth and sixth grade rooms were then on the left, just before the principal's office and the front entrance to the school.

Now, that is the grammar school side. The high school side was similar. As you looked at the school from the back again, the twelfth-grade room was the first room on the right, as you went in the back door. That was followed by the eleventh, tenth, and ninth grade rooms. As you rounded the corner, the eighth and seventh grade rooms were on the right, just before the front entrance to the school.

If you came in the front entrance to the school, straight in front of you was what was called the auditorium. Registration was held in this huge room and all big activities took place here. It was also used for basketball games, and all play periods (grammar school), and PE (physical education – high school), when the weather did not permit outside play.

After registration, they had a little get-together for everybody with refreshments and all. It turned out that our earlier issues weren't that much different from several of the other mother's issues. They all stood around and laughed about their dilemmas that took place before they got there. However, I do think that, if there had been awards given, Mama would have won first place.

Registration had gone about like Mama had planned, way back on Sunday. She went over to the desk to see where the first-grade room was, and then we went out the back of the auditorium and into the back of the school to the first grade.

Boy, were we surprised when we walked in the room and there stood Mrs. Claxton. You remember the preacher, Pastor Claxton? Well, his wife was to be my teacher. It was good to see my teacher was somebody I knew. Now, I wouldn't have to break her in. She was already broke in. I was beginning to feel a whole lot better about this school thing.

There was one lady and her son, who was standing over to the side, already there. So, Mrs. Claxton started talking with all of us about the things we would be doing and where we would sit and everything like that. You know, general stuff. But then she wanted to know what all I knew, and what I could do, as far as schoolin' goes. Well, that conversation didn't take long at all.

Me and this other kid was just kinda standing over to the side, so I said, "My name is Kerry. Like Kerry Drake in the funny papers." He laughed and said his mama read that to him every Sunday.

I said mine did too, and we laughed about that. We was doing a lot of laughing. His name was Cyrus Motes, and I pretty much liked him right off. He was about my size and real friendly.

While we was talking about different things and stuff, in walked this girl with her mama. Well, we just stopped talking and looked. When her mama started talking to Mrs. Claxton and my Mama, she just came right over to us and said, "Hi!"

Just like that! "Hi!"

Well, we didn't know what to say, so we just stood there and didn't say anything. I mean, what do you say? A strange girl walks right up to you and says, "Hi!"

Do you know what she did next? She said, "My name is Cara Blackthorn. Do either one of you talk?"

I started feeling kinda strange. My mind was working too fast. Things started looking fuzzy. Then.........

All of a sudden, I wasn't who I was anymore. I was somebody else. I was, "Danger Man!" If there was any danger around, I could smell it out, and when I did, I became "Danger Man!"

If ever there was danger, there was danger here. It was stalking around this room like she, uh, like it was in charge. I tried to warn Cyrus, but he was not honed in on it like me. He was still a rookie, but I would bring him along slowly. He was appearing a little timid, but I would teach him just how to handle these types.

My aim was to catch her off guard.

So, very sternly, I walked up to her and looked her, uh looked it, squarely in the eyes and said, nothing.

Again, being very pushy, she repeated, "I said Hi. My name is Cara Blackthorn. Do either one of you talk?"

I could tell she was trying to hide her fear, but she wasn't fooling me any. I'd seen her kind before, and I was not about to give her time to recover. This next move would really throw her off her game.

Immediately, feeling very confident, I marched right over to my mama and said, "Is it time to go, yet?"

She said it was, and started telling the other ladies bye, and how they would get together soon. I thought, "Not if I have anything to do with it." I could sense an eerie presence in the room. I felt a giant conspiracy forming in this room as we prepared to leave.

Slowly I started turning back into my old self. I waved bye to Cyrus who was looking a bit pale from watching my performance, and whats-her-name was obviously in awe, also. It had been a very successful venture into my alter ego, "Danger Man!"

On the way back to the auditorium, Mama said she felt real good about Mrs. Claxton, and said she knew I was going to do real good in her class. Me? Now I wasn't feeling as good about this school thing as I was before. I mean, nobody told me I was going to have to be with girls.

On the way back home, Mama asked what I thought about school now. I asked her why nobody told me there was going to be girls in my room. You know what she said? "Well, you better get used to 'em big boy, 'cause comin' next Tuesday, there will be even more of 'em. Next Monday is Labor Day, and Tuesday is the first day of school."

Chapter Thirty-Three

Preparing for The Good 'ol Days of School

"Now," I was thinking, "Let me get this straight in my mind. I have four days between now and Tuesday to completely change my plans in life. No more having all day to figure out if I was going to ride my bike, or go jump in the water hole, or play with 'ol Sue. No more running in the house in the middle of the day and asking Mama for a peanut butter and jelly sandwich. No more running by Rosa, pulling her hair, and then running out the door with her chasing me. And worst of all, no more going down to Isaiah's and catching frogs out back of his house."

Ahh! The good old days of school. Go Figure!

Now, it would all be figured out for me. But I wasn't sure how that was going to work out. All day Friday, all I did was lay around the house and worry about what that girl was going to do. Should I get out now while the getting was good? (Where'd that thought come from? I don't even know what that means.)

All of a sudden, I knew what to do. I'll go to the one who is the smartest of all. The one I have always been able to count on. The one who has been around the block and back. The one who has had years of experience in life.

My big brother, Timmy!

So, off I went in search of Timmy. I went to our bedroom, but no Timmy. I went to the living room, but no Timmy. I went out back to the barn, but still, no Timmy.

Hmm! Where would he be? Where would my genius big brother be? I walked back through the house and shazam! There he was, sitting on the kitchen table picking stuff out from between his toes.

Fascinated, I sat down to watch what he might fish out from in there, when Mama comes in and sees him up there. She grabbed the broom and chased us both out of the house with me trying to tell her all I was doing was watching. I wasn't picking. She wasn't interested in anything I had to say. Again, go figure.

Well, after running around the house twice, we finally stopped running in the front yard by the tree swing.

We just sat down with our backs up against the tree trying to get our breath. Our mama was quite a runner, but we were starting to get to where we could wear her down.

After a bit, I told Timmy about my problem and asked him why he didn't think to tell me about girls being in my class. He just looked at me and said, "Did 'ol Sue kick you in the head or what?"

I asked him why he would say that, and he said, "Look kid, let me fill you in and give you the benefit of all my years of experience and wisdom." "Life," he said, "Is full of all kinds of roads. There's dirt roads and paved roads. Straight roads and crooked roads. Roads that go up hills and roads that go down hills." (This was starting to sound awfully familiar.)

So, I stopped him right there and asked him what that had to do with my problem. He just stopped and looked kinda thoughtful. That was a look that was strange to him.

He then told me that having girls in the room might not be all that bad. He said there might even be some advantages to it. I started thinking that Sue must have kicked him in the head.

He said that, on the rare occasions that I might get into some kind of trouble, it was always good to have someone else there to blame it on. That's what girls are there for.

I asked him if that was what he always did and he said he never had to worry about it, because that was what he had Rosa there for. Now, I was starting to feel a whole lot better about it. My big brother had come through again. What a mind!

Well, that shore helped me be able to relax and enjoy the next three days of freedom. I jumped and ran and did what ever it was that crossed my mind. That is, except for the times when Mama would slap me behind the ear, or when she would hit me with the broom, or pick me up and put me under the sink in the kitchen where she could watch me. After a bit being under there, I would go to sleep, and she would forget all about me even being there. That was the agravat'en part.

Now, come Sunday morning we all got our new clothes on and went to church. I had to try to be on my best behavior for Mrs. Claxton, but it wasn't always possible. For the first time I did notice that there were girls in there and wondered why it hadn't bothered me before.

Anyway, when we were talking about where the Bible says for children to obey their parents, she asked me if I was having any problems with that. I told her I wasn't have any problems with that, but my parents might be.

She asked me what I meant by that. I told I believed I might have a hearing problem and she asked why I would say that. I said because my mama is all the time saying, "Can you not hear? I told you to stop doing that." I suggested that she start talking louder and she hit me on the ear, and I wondered if there might be a connection there. Anyway, I told her I didn't have a problem with obeying them when I heard them. Well, she just grabbed me and hugged me and almost cried. (I was thinking I might have just got a leg up on the first grade.)

So, after church we were walking out and Mama was holding my hand to keep me from running off. Mrs. Claxton stopped us and asked Mama if they'd ever had my hearing checked. Mama told her they hadn't, and why was she asking.

Mrs. Claxton informed her about our little talk in Sunday School and Mama told her that they were glad to know that, and would be sure to see to my hearing needs. When we got home, believe me Mama saw to it that my hearing was all cleared up. Boy, grownups have absolutely no sense of humor.

Chapter Thirty-Four

Labor Day
(Last day of freedom)

"It was Monday, September 4, 1950." According to *Dragnet*, "It was a warm and sunny day in Winterboro, Alabama. We were working the daywatch in arson investigations. My partner is Detective Timmy, and my name is Sargeant Drake."

"We were on stakeout next to a pit that was obviously dug for the purpose of building a fire, since there was a fire in it. We noticed that there were some logs burning in the pit and a grill had been placed over it. Someone had gone to a lot of trouble trying to disguise this pit, making it seem like there was some sort of cookout about to take place. We suspected there was something mighty fishy afoot here."

"Kerry, would you please stop with the mystery detective crap," interrupted Timmy. Daddy had told us to watch the fire while he would go in to get the meat. I didn't see what it would hurt if we played a little cops and robber stuff while we waited. So, I just poked Timmy in the side and said, "Stick'em up!"

Well Timmy, being very ticklish, slapped out at me and made my foot slip on the edge of the pit. Down went my feet into the fire. I screamed for help and Timmy, being the good big brother he is, started pulling me out. However, not before both my shoes, my brand-new shoes, had caught on fire.

We started beating on my shoes with pieces of wood trying to put them out. We didn't know that new shoes had lots of leather oil and other flammable stuff on them. We quickly put out the fire on both shoes, but not before they were pretty much scorched up.

I'm figuring that by now you've already learned that every time somebody screams in our family, everybody comes running. Well, this time was no exception.

Daddy, Mama, Bertha Lou, Lora Lee and Rosa Sharon, all came bustin' out that back door to see what was the matter.

When they got to the pit, they stopped. The look on all their faces told the whole story. Daddy, who was holding the long fork used for sticking the meat, looked at my shoes, then looked at me. Then looked at my shoes. Then looked at me. Slowly, with smoke coming out of his ears, he started raising the fork. Mama, seeing the look in his eyes, grabbed his arm and shouted, "Vernon, No!"

While Mama was crying, Daddy's brain was frying, and everybody else was giggling. Mama wanted to know, why in this world, I had my new shoes on. (Daddy, still all red in the face, wanted to know why I still had my feet on.) I told her it was because I liked them so much. Well, that kinda got to her and she calmed down a mite. Then, with some of the pained look gone from her face, she smiled and said Daddy would now have to make me some new shoe bottoms. She said that would have to do 'til they could get me some new shoes. I tried to tell them it was Timmy's fault, but nobody wanted to hear anything I had to say. Timmy just grinned.

Later, as we sat down around the picnic table, the only thing hotter than the meat on that platter was my rear-end. The shoes were ruined. The burning oil and leather conditioner, and other stuff caused the shoes to shrivel up and die.

But, now I'm here to tell you, that was a feast fit for kings. Mama and the girls had just done themselves proud with baked beans, tater salad, and deviled eggs. (I didn't understand that name, though. Deviled eggs? I guess it was the cuttin'em open and then fillin'em up again, like the preacher said Jesus did for us.)

I hate to say it, but I had done a job on that pit. After caving in one side and strewing burning wood everywhere, Daddy had to fix the sides all up again. He got another fire going and then grilled up that chicken real nice. He lathered on some really good sauce all over it that Mama had made. She called it her barbeque sauce and I couldn't help it, but I got it pretty much all over me. Mama said that was alright though 'cause I had to get a bath anyway. (I don't know why people has to throw in things like that right in the middle of having a good time.) Daddy also grilled hamburgers, and hotdogs. We figured we'd be eating on all this food for days to come.

After all the cleaning up had been done, we were all sitting out in the yard drinking iced tea and talking about school starting tomorrow and all the things we needed to do to get ready.

Well, I wanted to talk about something else. I figured if I could talk enough, they'd think how cute I was, and forget all about what I'd done earlier.

So, I asked Daddy why they called today "Labor Day." He didn't say anything. Mama said, real loud, "Vernon!" Daddy jumped, mumbled something, then just looked around. Mama said his mind was "owchunder" in the field somewhere. I don't think he had fully recovered from the earlier mishap.

So, I asked again, "Daddy, why do they call this "Labor Day?" He just kinda looked around, mumbled a little with some ums and uhs, then said, "Well, let me see now. It all started a good long while ago." He went on to say how it used to be that people didn't have any rights at all as far as work goes. All the business owners and landowners told the workers when they were to start working and when they could quit working. Basically that was from daylight to dark."

He said, "They also only paid them the least they could get by with. That was such a little amount that the people even had to make their own children go to work in order to help pay for food for the family."

"Well, when the people started talking about not going to work, the owners were forced into raising their pay. But it was still a bad situation." "Finally," Daddy said, "The government came up with laws that said how much the workers would get paid so the workers could live and pay their bills and buy food. The workers could even change jobs if they could find one that paid more." This meant that the children started being able to go to school.

"So, Kerry," Daddy said, "This is the day that the government passed the new labor laws, and they called it "Labor Day." Now it's celebrated every year by giving everyone a day off to be with their families. Now, wasn't that nice?"

"But, Daddy," I said. "All of that was well and good if you was a grownup. But, if you was a kid, you then had to start going to school with girls." Everybody just laughed and laughed about that. But me!

After most everybody had gone in, I went over to Mama and Daddy and told them how sorry I was for tearing up my new shoes and everything. I told them I didn't know why, but when everybody else was regular, I was always stepping in something. They just looked down at me, smiled and said everything was alright. Daddy said it was natural for little boys to mess up a lot, so that when they got big, all that messing up would be all out of them.

Mama said not to worry about it, and that she would get me some more new shoes. She said it would probably take a couple of weeks to get here. Then they both got down and gave me great, big hugs. Boy, maybe grownups do have a sense of humor after-all.

Chapter Thirty-Five

Going to School

(Nothing Could Go Wrong Here, Right?)

Well, the next morning was about as hectic as it could possibly be. Daddy had taken off half a day to help Mama get us all ready and off to school. They had laid out all of our clothes and shoes last night for us to get dressed as quickly and correctly as we could.

When I saw my shoes, I was so surprised. My old shoes looked brand new. Daddy had spent a lot of time washing and polishing them to a great shine.

He had even already put new bottoms in them. He told me to be careful and to watch where I walk so as not to step in any water or mud because it would ruin the cardboard. I told him I would be very careful. He gave me a funny look, shook his head, and went to the kitchen. I heard him mumbling something to Mama about a brick wall, but I figured he was just planning on building something. He's always got a project going.

When we were all dressed, Mama called us into the kitchen. She said it was for "inspection." I didn't know what that was, but figured it was to check us out. She looked us all up and down, one by one. Everybody got a, "…that's real good," except me.

Mama said, "Kerry, did Timmy dress you?"

Well, I didn't want to him to get all the credit, so I just said, "He helped me a little bit, Mama. But I did most of it, myself," I said proudly.

She told me to come there and said, "Look down and tell me what you see."

I stuck my chest out and said, "My new-looking shoes. Ain't they pretty?"

"What's wrong with them," she asked.

I looked again and said, "Uh, did he paint them the wrong color?"

"He didn't paint them at all you, uh, son. He polished them. But you have them on the wrong feet."

"But Mama, these are the only feet I got. Hey, are these Timmy's feet?"

"No, they are not Timmy's feet, Kerry," Mama said, sounding kinda flusterated. (I figured since I was going to school, I needed to start using bigger words."

"You need to swap them around. Put this one on this foot, and put this one on this foot," she said pointing to my feet.

"Oh, ok," I said as I began to do that. I was wondering why she didn't just say that to start with. I'm not stupid, or nothin'.

"Now then Kerry, turn around." I turned around and she said, "You have your overall straps crossed. Here, let fix them for you."

All the while this has been going on, the others have been going out, one at a time, covering their mouths and shaking. Something in there must have been making them sick. I couldn't tell what it was 'cause I was too busy trying to get ready for school.

While we was getting dressed, Mama had been fixin' our breakfasts and Daddy had been fixin' our lunches to take to school. We all had Oatmeal, buttered toast, and milk for breakfast. All of our lunches were balony samiches with mustard and pickle, and a banana. We also had a nickel for milk. For our mid-morning break, we had an apple. Boy, we were really fixed up. I couldn't wait for lunch.

Well, here I am ready to get on the bus to go to my very first day, of my very first year of school. It's going to be a really adventurous time in my life. I have a new teacher, a new friend, a new girlfriend, and a really new world waiting for me here.

Won't you come back to experience all of this new world with me?

ABOUT THE AUTHOR

Kerry was born January 30, 1944 in Leeds, Alabama. He was the last of eight children, the first two having died very early in life. Then, as the book describes, after moving around a bit, they moved to Childersburg where he grew up in this wonderful small town. Here, he had the best of all worlds, a great family, a great community, and the most precious of friends. Friends that have lasted a lifetime.

In the summer before his senior year, there was a terrible flood in Childersburg and he was inspired by the extraordinary work of the National Guard. He saw them doing so many things, for so many people. He was unavoidably moved and felt a strong desire, so he joined the National Guard.

After graduation the next year, he left for Fort Jackson, South Carolina for six months active-duty Basic Training and then Advanced Individual Training (AIT). He stayed in the National Guard for six years, with the last two years in a large unit in Jefferson County being a Drill Sergeant E5 preparing men for combat.

When he came home from basic training and AIT duty, he enrolled in college majoring in math and computer sciences. After graduating, he went to work for a large iron manufacturing company as a junior operator in their computer operations department. It was an early generation computer operation.

After a few years, as operations supervisor, he was responsible for the payroll, accounts payable and accounts receivable, for the main company and four subsidiaries in Alabama and Texas. In seven years, he took the department through a number of computer generation growth levels.

After a number of years, he saw that a paper manufacturing conglomerate was about to buy out the iron company and close it down (for tax purposes). He then accepted an offer as sales and marketing manager for a commercial supply company.

Through his leadership, this company experienced significant growth. However, after realizing that he missed the computer world, he accepted an offer for operations manager from a data processing service bureau.

This involved overseeing computer work for other companies in town, in state and in other states. They would send the finished work back to the companies in either paper format, punched card, or magnetic tape. There was also extensive travel time involved with other companies, in and out of state.

After a few years, he was offered a position with The Southern Company at its huge operations facility in Mountain Brook. This operations facility was under ground and had state-of-the-art computers that controlled the flow of electricity throughout the states of Alabama, Florida, Georgia and Mississippi. It was among the highest in security and secrecy in the southeast.

Sometimes, a highly motivated person can think too much of himself and make a bad decision. This came when he saw what he thought was a chance to buy, build, and run his own business. So, he left The Southern Company and after putting everything he had into this business, he saw it fail. This was not a good time.

But, as Romans 8:28 says, "...all things work together for good to those who love God, those who are called for His purpose." Also, 8:31, "….if God is for us, who could ever be against us?"

After being a beneficiary of Kerry's attributes in the business world and learning of his availability, the owner of an industrial service and supply company called and offered him a position as Sales and Marketing Director of his multimillion-dollar business. It covered Jefferson County. He then, through his previous contacts, was able to grow this business even more. The largest account (over one million dollars/yr) was The Birmingham News. While with this company he started a city wide, then state wide, courier service subsidiary.

What's the quote from Longfellow? "Into each life some rain must fall."

After a few years, the owner announced that he was retiring and for tax purposes he would close down the business. Kerry and others tried to buy it, but to no avail. This put over 100 people out of work.

So, it was from this, some might say a knee buckler, came the most satisfying and rewarding time of his business life. By the will of God, and the influence of a friend, he was able to get on at UAB. He started out at the lowest research job there at $5.50/hr. in the Nutrition Sciences Department. This was mammory cancer research. Working with rats. No joke. He would be experimenting with different diets to see what effects, if any, it would have on tumors.

Dr. Clinton Grubbs told him that he derived all his money from government grants and that was why he could only start him out at that amount. He did say that UAB (at that time) gave an automatic raise to everyone at their sixth month anniversary.

He added, "If you do good, consistent work, when another position comes open in the university, I will do all I can to help you get it."

However, Kerry, being a quick study, was able to receive a raise after three months in addition to his six month's raise. By the end of the first year Kerry was doing all the chemistry analysis work for the experiments.

After two and a half years, a world-renown cardiologist, Dr. Garreth Roubin came from Emory University to UAB. His expertise was in Interventional Cardiology, and he was going to start a research cath lab, the first at UAB, and needed help.

Dr. Grubbs, true to his word, told Kerry about this new physician looking for help and asked him if he wanted to interview for the job. Naturally, he said, "Yes."

Well, to make a long story short, he got the job. He tasked Kerry, and a young Cardiology Fellow, Brad Cavander, to take an old x-ray room, that was now just a filthy storage room, and convert it into a cath lab capable of performing sterile cath procedures. Within two months they were doing sterile cath procedures.

At the beginning Dr. Roubin, in order for Kerry to learn the procedures himself, had him come to the hospital cath lab and observe everything concerning coronary cath procedures.

So, there he was, his very first procedure, standing beside the table next to Dr. Roubin. As he was all scrubbed up as required, he began to see the seriousness of all of this. There, with all the monitors around them, as well as all the other medical personnel, the initial injection of contrast was administered to the patient.

Then suddenly, someone at a console over in the corner shouted, "FIB!" Kerry, in his ignorance, just thought someone was going to tell a joke, or something. That was when a nurse came up, handed Dr. Roubin some paddles and the patient was shocked back into normal heart rhythm.

Well, needless to say, Kerry broke out in a cold sweat, knees started buckling, and he had to be helped to a chair. He found himself wondering, "What in the world have I gotten myself into now?"

For the next twelve years Kerry performed over one thousand balloon cath procedures with stent implants. Most were coronary stents, but there were also brain stents, renal (kidney) artery stents, femoral artery stents, carotid artery stents, abdominal aorta stents, and others. He was honored to be guest teacher at a number of universities in other states on the techniques of stent deployment.

He attained to the position of Director and Research Coordinator of Interventional Cardiology Research Laboratories.

Kerry also trained a lot of new Cardiology Fellows to do these stent implant procedures. Dr. Roubin wanted his new cardiologists to know what the procedure was all about before coming into the clinical cath lab.

He also trained cardiologists from other countries such as, China, Taiwan, Hungary, Poland, England, France, South Korea, Sweden, India, Pakistan, Australia, and others.

Oh, I forgot to tell you. Kerry's patients were pigs. 100 pound pigs. As most everyone now knows, the pig cardiovascular system is very similar to the human system.

Everything that was done in the hospital cath lab, was performed exactly the same way in the research cath lab, from anesthesia to recovery. (Except for grabbing a 100 pound violently powerful swine by the hind leg and injecting it in the hip.)

Kerry did most of the pre-clinical research on the first coronary stent to receive approval by the FDA on humans in the United States. He was also responsible for writing the research protocols and submitting them for approval to the FDA and NIH.

The most humbling of all would be when Dr. Roubin would sometimes have Kerry accompany him to the patient's rooms after their stent implants. He was able to see the patients up and walking around for the first time in a long time. Then Dr. Roubin would tell them that Kerry was responsible for the research of the stent they had received.

After the construction of state-of-the-art cath labs in the hospital, along with training facilities for the new fellows, the research cath lab at UAB came to a halt. Kerry was then tasked to learn and perform, then teach, micro-surgery heart transplant techniques in mice.

The purpose of this study was to learn to manipulate the genes in order to prevent human organ transplant rejection. (Look at the fingernail of a five-year-old child and you get the idea of the size of a mouse's heart.) This had never been done at UAB. Kerry would take the heart from one mouse and transplant it into the abdomen of another mouse, making all the necessary vascular connections. The new heart would then start beating simultaneously with the mouse's own heart. Again, you can understand Kerry being invited to teach these techniques at other universities.

After twenty years He retired from UAB with a very nice reception party that was attended by many cardiologists, surgeons, nurses and technicians.

Especially in attendance was then retired, Dr. Clinton Grubbs, to whom He owes everything. Also, some of his classmates and friends from Childersburg were in attendance.

Well, to sum it all up, Kerry has done a few things. His mama said one time, "Kerry, can't you just stick with one job? Your daddy and brothers worked a long time at one job."

Let's see now: School boy; Soldier; Degrees in Computer operations and Computer Science; Sales and Marketing; Computer Science and Operations for an Electric Utility; Medical Science Investigator and research author; and now, a book. Boy, he just couldn't keep a job. He's sorry, Mama.

But his proudest achievement is marrying the most wonderful, beautiful, patient, and sweetest woman in the whole world, and having four beautiful children. Without God and Joyce, he could not have done anything.

CPSIA information can be obtained
at www.ICGtesting.com
Printed in the USA
BVHW070040161222
654335BV00017B/1245

9 798885 907859